"The good news is that your parents died very wealthy.
The bad news is they left it in trust."

PANKAUSKI's TRUSTEE'S GUIDE

10 Steps to
Family Trustee Excellence

JOHN PANKAUSKI

AuthorHouse™
1663 Liberty Drive
Bloomington, IN 47403
www.authorhouse.com
Phone: 1 (800) 839-8640

Published by AuthorHouse 4/1/2015

ISBN: 978-1-5049-0333-2 (sc)
ISBN: 978-1-5049-0207-6 (hc)

Library of Congress Control Number: 2015904991

Print information available on the last page.

This book is printed on acid-free paper.

To Mom and Dad

Who made everything possible

"Never Idle a Minute"

Disclaimer

The concepts throughout this book are based on general principles of trusts and the administration of trusts, and are not intended to be an exhaustive list of all of the issues you may confront while serving as trustee. This book will not answer all of your questions or tell you what to do each step of the way. A book cannot replace competent trust counsel nor an experienced co-trustee. The laws which govern the administration of a trust vary from time to time, from state to state, and evolve. Although some legal issues recur, each matter or administration issue is different. Some of the principles discussed in this book may not be applicable to you, or to the trust you are involved with. While examples are used throughout this book, perspective, opinions, and results will vary from one jurisdiction to the next. In a nutshell: I hope that this book provides some insight and guidance for you, whether deciding to serve as trustee, or not, or learning of potential pitfalls and traps, and best practices. But it can't replace a competent experienced trust attorney familiar with your jurisdiction and governing laws.

Preface

Congratulations!

You've been named a trustee and can't wait to begin to serve, right? Not so fast.

If you have visions of being in control of money, making important decisions, investing, and telling beneficiaries "no," then here are some words of caution: look before you leap and be careful what you wish for.

> **$59 Trillion is being transferred
> – right now! –
> from the WWII generation to the
> Baby-Boomers, and Gens X and Y,
> much of it in trust. Are you ready?**

Being a trustee is serious business, with serious potential liability for the unwary, the uninformed, and the uncooperative.

After all, you're dealing with individual, personal issues such as the care, support, maintenance and lifestyles of beneficiaries. You'll decide what will be distributed, or not, for such things as education, health, insurance, medical bills, electric bills, maintenance of one's residence, real estate taxes, and other items. Before you begin your trusteeship, consider why you want to serve, and if you decide that you want to, consider the issues raised in this book.

The purpose of this book is to educate an individual who is serving or is going to serve as the trustee of a trust. It is meant to be educational, informative, easy to read, and in plain English. This book is also a wakeup call for those who may misunderstand what their role as a trustee should be.

Why is this book worth your money and time? Three reasons. First, we are in the middle of a massive, unprecedented wealth transfer from the WWII generation to the Baby Boomers occurring right now! Millions. Billions. Trillions in real estate, brokerage accounts, homes, IRAs, gold, heirlooms, artwork, intellectual property, and other valuables are being transferred. Second, here's a reality check: much of that wealth will not be given to beneficiaries outright. Rather, it will have financial handcuffs on it: it will be in a trust. Most people not only have a will, and some joint accounts, but also a revocable or living trust. The revocable trust has increasingly become the main dispositive vehicle for one's wealth. These trusts will become irrevocable after the death of the trust creator, and will continue to exist and to manage the wealth held in the trust for the benefit of third parties, beneficiaries.

Much wealth will be held in trust for nieces, nephews, surviving spouses, children, grandchildren and loved ones.

Some will be managed, and mis-managed, used and abused, misappropriated, mis-distributed, wasted and squandered to in-laws, outlaws, mistresses and misfits, ne'er-do-wells, the lazy and lucky, the incompetent and un-deserving. Are you ready?

Along with this massive wealth shift, there is a third reason: family disharmony. Although you may be connected to some one by DNA, blood or marriage, you may not get along with them. Disharmony and disdain are common when money is at issue. Take a family that may have differences, and add a second or third marriage, in-laws and step-children, throw in lots of money and property and now you've got a potential powder keg among disagreeing family members. The trust is the stage for everyone to act out on.

Although this book will prove helpful to employees of trust companies and trust departments of financial institutions, as well as paralegals and attorneys new to the fiduciary world, it is, nonetheless, directed toward an individual, such as a family member, who is serving as trustee. You are probably a close friend or family member of the person who created a trust. You may view being a trustee as a sense of service to a loved one or a deceased family member. At the very least, you are an advisor or a person in whom great confidence is placed. This book is a guidepost for the individual trustee, and will cover the basic concepts that you will want to consider, reflect on, and grasp, hopefully before you begin to serve, but certainly during your tenure, as trustee.

Hopefully, you will be a good trustee. Regardless, I'm going to demonstrate how good persons can be poor trustees. And how bad trustees get into trouble. A lot of trouble.

Why is it important to understand how to be a good trustee and how to avoid errors of bad trustees? Well, most of us would agree that if we are going to do anything, then it's worth doing it correctly. But there's a more selfish reason for you to understand what it means to be a good trustee. You face serious liability if you're a poor trustee, if you act improperly, make mistakes or, God forbid, act in an arbitrary or nasty way to the trust beneficiaries.

You may be liable for monetary damages. Those damages for being a poor trustee will be paid by you personally – damages will not come from the trust.

> If you think this is overly dramatic,
> please think again.
> If you think that that is not accurate,
> please think again.

I'm a trust litigator. My law firm limits its practice to estate, trust, and guardianship litigation and administration matters. This is all we do and we see individual trustees behaving poorly or badly on a regular basis. Most of time, the poor trustees don't even know they are doing it; or they are in denial.

If balancing personal interests and situations of the beneficiaries were not enough, serving as trustee also requires extreme focus and discipline regarding money: the world of investing combines with management of property, along with decisions of administration and prudent conduct.

To put it bluntly, many individual trustees get into a lot of trouble. You mismanage trust assets or invest them improperly. You ignore the plain language of the trust document and fail to understand or ascertain the intent of the trust. You treat the trust assets as your own and impose your personal feelings, beliefs, dissatisfactions and animosities when you should be objective, prudent and unbiased.

By all accounts, individuals – not just corporate institutions or banks – serving as trustee is common, increasing, and even explosive due to the use of the revocable trust in one's estate plan. Trusts are no longer sophisticated techniques for only the wealthy, but are now considered common and basic parts of an individual's estate plan. Even the most meager of clients have a checking account, an IRA or retirement account, some mutual funds, a vehicle, a dwelling, and personal property. Many of these assets, and much of Americans' wealth ("stuff") are being held, administered, distributed, and not distributed in trust.

> Everyone is using trusts to hold, manage, administer and pass along, wealth for everyone including outlaws, in-laws, mistresses and misfits along with the "normal" beneficiaries such as surviving spouses, children, heirs, next of kin and loved ones

Introduction

Understanding the Basics: Learning the Language and Who the Legal Actors Are

You need to know what, and who, surrounds your role as a trustee.

Administering a trust is not inheriting money. If you don't understand what you are getting into, you either need to hire someone who does, or decline to serve, or, if you have already started serving, resign.

Even though you are entitled to compensation, money is no reason to serve.

People want to control things from the grave. When people die, they don't want to just throw a bunch of money in a beneficiary's lap. Most of this money is not unrestricted. It is restricted. It's in trust.

When people ask me to describe my law practice, I often de scribe it as a boutique firm with a small group of very talented professionals, fighting over "blood and money". We not only advocate, and argue, about the silverware and

Shih Tzu, but mom, millions, mistresses, and mentality. We deal with war ring spouses and ex-spouses, sibling rivalry, petty jealousies, and childhood grudges played out by adults who are decades older, but no more mature.

In many of these situations, I hear about family "issues". It makes me think that part of my job is to be a wealth psychologist. I joke with my good colleague, trustee and guardian extraordinaire, Jacqueline Chiodo, who holds a masters in psychology, that she is better equipped to handle co-trustees, trust beneficiaries, family members, than Wharton MBAs are.

Controlling from the grave

It's your job, as trustee, to objectively, and fairly determine who gets the money—and who doesn't. You can't screw this up. If you don't have the stomach or aptitude for this, there are options: hire a professional or resign.

Many well-intentioned individuals wish to appoint a family member or loved one, typically someone they know, and trust, to be in charge of their trust. This book makes that assumption: that you have been asked to serve as trustee, or you have been "appointed" trustee in a trust document, by someone you know. It may be your spouse, your mother or father, or best friend.

Often, when money and property is left in trust, there are individuals who want to control it. Control freaks. They ask to be trustee or seek out their appointment as trustee or otherwise gladly accept an appointment without hesitation. These are the ones who get into some of the most trouble.

Here is the ugly truth: Most individuals do not have the experience or time to properly administer a trust, let alone prudently invest the assets. They need guidance. At the risk of sounding self-serving, the truth is that the single best thing that an individual can do prior to serving as trustee is to hire a competent trust attorney who has years of experience in trust administration. The second-best thing that a trustee can do is hire a competent trust company as investment agent or co-trustee. The third best thing that they can do is read, and reread, the trust document. The fourth best thing? You probably have it figured out: if the first three don't work—resign.

Being a trustee is not for everyone. If you don't have the time or experience, consider passing, or hiring a co-trustee and trust counsel, and delegating investment authority to a professional.

The best decision you might make may be the one to walk away.

It is best to start off with an understanding of what and who you will encounter and their significance to the trust. There are many "legal actors" you will encounter during your trusteeship and many concepts and procedures which may be new. A basic understanding, or background is often helpful.

Beneficiaries: those who may receive the benefits of the trust property and for whom the trustee administers the trust.

Income beneficiaries: beneficiaries for whom the trustee may, or shall, distribute the income which is produced by trust assets such as interest and dividends.

Lifetime beneficiaries: those who may benefit from the trust during their own lifetime.

Life estate: the right to use, occupy or enjoy some property for your life, after which the property is distributed to a pre-determined recipient.

Remainder beneficiaries: refer to those who take a later interest in the trust, typically after the death of another, or a prior, beneficiary, such as a lifetime beneficiary.

Discretionary beneficiary: Who is eligible, but not necessarily entitled, to receive distributions of principal or income, as the trustee determines in the exercise of its discretion.

Settlor: The creator of the trust, also referred to as a **"grantor."**

Decedent: A person who has passed away or died. The settlor of a trust is often referred to as a decedent when that settlor passes.

Trustee: is the manager of the trust—a fiduciary who is charged with looking out for and protecting the trust property for the benefit of the beneficiaries. Think of the trustee as a selfless cop, a doctor, an investor, a manager, all wrapped up into one.

Trust: is an entity, much like a corporation. It is a living, breathing thing which has its own existence separate and distinct from the trustee or the beneficiaries. It must file tax returns and it has its own unique legal identity and existence. It is also a relationship, created by the settler and accepted by the trustee, for the benefit of the beneficiaries.

Trust agreement or ***trust document (or deed or declaration of trust):*** The writing which creates the trust. A trust's bylaws or governing rules are reflected in the trust document, which is the writing which creates the trust. The written trust document, including any valid amendments, constitute the entire trust agreement.

Amendments: The trust agreement may have additional written changes, when the trust, by its terms, permits changes. For example, while a client is alive, he or she may execute amendments to their revocable trust, or may republish or restate it in its entirety. Most states require that a trust be in writing and signed at the end of the document by the grantor and two witnesses.

Oral trusts or ***constructive trusts:*** The law does recognize certain specific types of non-written trusts, which are not the subject of this book.

Revocable trust: Has also been referred to as a ***living trust*** or a ***revocable living trust***. It may be revoked or changed by the grantor during the grantor's lifetime and while the grantor is competent.

Irrevocable trust: May not be changed or revoked.

Testamentary trust: Created upon the death of the grantor, typically contained in the language of a will, sometimes referred to as a *testamentary trust created under will*.

Life insurance trust: Irrevocable trust which is owner and beneficiary of a life insurance policy, typically on grantor's life. Often referred to as an *ILIT* (irrevocable life insurance trust.)

Dynasty trust: Refers to a multigenerational trust which can support one's children and grandchildren and more remote descendants for decades and even centuries.

Trust protector: An amorphous term attributed to a legal actor who is not the trustee, but who has been given certain authority by the grantor. The trust protector may be appointed by the grantor to monitor the trustee for the exclusive benefit of one or more beneficiaries or may have the right to remove and replace a trustee, or to expand or eliminate the beneficiaries' interest in the trust.

Corpus or *res:* the property which is held by or is in the trust.

Governing law: The law of the state or country which is applied to the interpretation or administration of the trust and which determines rights and responsibilities of the trustee and beneficiaries.

Income and *principal:* Two categories of trust assets. Principal assets are the properties which the trust holds and comprise the corpus, such as bonds, stocks and real estate. Income is what is generated by principal assets, such as dividends, interest and rents.

Personal representative: A fiduciary who administers an estate, also referred to as an executor. (or administrator).

Simple or *pour over will:* A short will which appoints the personal representative, identifies family members and then leaves property (which "pours over") to the person's revocable trust.

Venue: Determining which state or county or which court may hear a trust dispute.

Construction action: A lawsuit asking a court to interpret, or construe, the terms of a trust, and tell you what a trust means or says. It has nothing to do with real estate or the construction industry.

Petition or *complaint:* Document filed by one initiating a lawsuit involving an estate or a trust.

Interested persons: Are those people who have a stake in the trust who may be affected by any action or litigation. They may include the trustee, grantor, all beneficiaries, and perhaps other third parties such as creditors and trust protectors.

Ascertainable standard: Recognized criteria for distribution of trust funds. The most common are health, education, maintenance and support.

Now, it's important to understand why you want to be a trustee.

"*My doctor says I should wait. But if I get them done now, my trust attorney says I get money from the trust because that's money for 'health'. And in five years when I want them freshened up, that's 'maintenance.'*"

Table of Contents

What's more important…

Blood or Money…?

1

Know Why You Are Serving As Trustee

You need to know, and understand, why you choose to serve.

Why in the world would you want to be a trustee?

Why...

- Would you want to deal with beneficiaries' demands for money, their insecurities and feelings of inadequacy? And their demons?

- Would you want to (indeed volunteer or agree) to account every year, review investment statements, deal with beneficiaries who may want to sue you, invest others' funds for income and yield and also capital appreciation, and, perhaps worst of all, deal with attorneys?

- Work in an environment where your every act is questioned and subject to Monday morning quarter-backing?

If you're holding a lot of cash and the markets go up, beneficiaries complain that you failed to capture those gains. If you're fully invested in the market and the market takes a dip, the beneficiaries complain that you are overexposed. If one of six beneficiaries requests funds for a minor child's education, the other five beneficiaries will want a similar distribution—regardless of need. A beneficiary who is monetarily successful or rich in her own right will demand that you not consider other financial resources when distributing trust funds to her. The beneficiary who is a schoolteacher or social worker will wonder why you are distributing trust funds to a beneficiary who is a successful doctor or lawyer.

Don't You Have Better Things To Do With Your Time?

Welcome to the world of being a trustee. Where your every act is questioned, and every beneficiary believes that they can do a better job than you can.

This chapter will ask you to think hard about why you want to serve as trustee, and provide some background or window dressing to the role. It will discuss recurring thoughts of your family members and how they may react to one's wealth and inheritances.

Being a trustee is a great responsibility. Perfection is not required, but incompetence shall not be tolerated. You must know what you are responsible for, to whom you owe duties, and how you must carry out those obligations. Being a trustee is not an easy task. It's serious business and definitely NOT for everyone.

The point is this: there is a lot more to being a trustee than understanding the financial markets or whether to purchase stocks or bonds. You need to recognize this. Understand it. Accept it. And act accordingly. You need to understand what you are in for, and why you want to serve.

Here's A Scary Thought – Anyone Can Be A Trustee

Legally, there is no educational or experience requirement for one to serve as trustee. There is no law which requires you to have a college degree, let alone a graduate degree in finance, accounting or law, to be eligible to serve as trustee. No statute or rule requires you to have, for example, 20 years of invest ing experience, or prior trust work. The only thing that is required is that you are competent, that is: of majority age and of sound mind.

A 90-year-old can be trustee. A felon could be a trustee. A Ponzi schemer can be a trustee. An entrepreneur with numerous failed ventures and bankruptcy filings can be a trustee. There is no IQ test or examination to pass. A neighbor can be trustee. There is no duration or time requirement: some trustees are nominated who have only known the grantor a matter of days. And there are no dollar limitations. That's right, the convicted felon who is nominated in a trust document to serve as trustee of a $250 Million trust can serve! What a country!

Realistically, do you really want someone with no understanding of investing, or a complete lack of experience with managing money, serving as the trustee of, say, a $5 Million trust? Of course not.

Ideally, you only want very experienced, knowledgeable, trust worthy, and intelligent persons serving as trustee. One can, however, make the argument that with the right counsel and investment agent, anyone with sound judgment can serve as trustee. Others would argue that that's hogwash. You should have a competent trustee on board first and foremost. If there are family members, beneficiaries, that you want involved with the trusts, there already exist a number of ways to have that person involved without serving as trustee. The final decision on who shall be a trustee should be more of a business decision, or a financial and administrative decision, than a personal or familial decision. Likewise, your decision to serve or not serve as trustee should make sense in more than a personal way to you.

Serving May Be Honorable, But At What Price? (Or Let's Blame The Attorneys)

Many times trustees who are embattled in trust litigation raise their swords, place on their armor, and stand like a knight, arguing that they are continuing service as trustee because that is what the grantor wanted. While sounding noble, this shortsighted assertion probably couldn't be further from the truth. It's doubtful the grantor would want you to serve as trustee had he or she known that litigation would result. The truth is that trustee selection is often a neglected part of the estate planning process. You were probably nominated to serve as trustee without much thought, without your consultation, but because you knew the grantor, and, quite frankly, he or she had no better alternatives.

When a client is preparing to create a trust, careful thought must go into who the client shall nominate to serve as trustee, both now, and in the future. The truth is that every day in every state across America, attorneys are drafting trusts and meeting with clients to discuss, or are failing to discuss, who shall, or should, be trustee. I see people who are appointed, who accept appointment, or who try to be installed as, trustee, who have no business serving in a fiduciary capacity. I see individuals who absolutely are the wrong choice for a trustee. Many lack experience. Most have no, or at most, a minimal desire to gain insight or intellect or experience in managing millions of dollars and serving as trustee. Why?

Much of the blame lies in the hands of the attorneys who fail to properly explain the role of the trustee to clients. Who else can adequately advise the client on how to carefully select a trustee and successor trustee? Far too often, attorneys, and even clients' financial and other advisors, fail to discuss possible scenarios of what a trust will look like when the client is gone. Or how a co-trustee or a successor trustee may act. Attorneys and other advisers fail to advise a client about the multitude of administration issues, pitfalls and traps for the unwary. And although I come down hard on attorneys, the truth is that much of the blame also needs to be attributed to the client. Most clients don't even speak to potential trustees to discuss with them whether they wish to serve as trustee, how they feel about that, and what their role would be. Likewise, little thought goes into how your trustee may interact with your beneficiaries.

Family Member As Trustee

Deciding to serve as trustee, even deciding to decline to serve, can become a challenge for family members who are nominated to serve. There is a natural inclination to want to accept the mantle of responsibility of the trust and to serve as trustee. This is particularly true of trusts where family members are not only a trustee but also a beneficiary. This is very common in trusts which benefit the surviving spouse. If you are a surviving spouse, and you just lost your husband or wife, who has left wealth to you in trust, wouldn't you want to be your own trustee? *Wanting* to be a trustee, is, however, quite different than being *competent* to serve as trustee.

The Successor

When a client creates a revocable trust, that client, the grantor of the trust, will customarily be his or her own trustee during lifetime. Why wouldn't you want to run your own trust, right? Upon the grantor's incapacity or death, a successor will take over. The successor will be that person named in the trust document who agrees to serve. If the named successor does not wish to serve, then the trust document may list the alternate, or other, successor trustees. If no one named in the trust document is willing or able to serve, then, depending on what the trust terms are, and what the governing law dictates, a court or the beneficiaries will appoint a successor trustee. There is a very common legal maxim that a trust shall not fail for want of a trustee.

You Can Decline To Serve

Here's the good news. You don't have to serve as trustee even if you are named. You can decline to serve. Merely sign a one page document which can be as brief as a sentence long, which states that you decline to serve. You need not give a reason. Deliver the declination, and a copy of the trust, including all original documents if you have any, to the successor trustee who is named in the trust document, and the beneficiaries. If there is no successor trustee named in the document, then you should notify all the beneficiaries in writing that you decline to serve and that they should retain counsel to protect their interests in the trust.

Resigning As Trustee

Resigning as trustee is a different issue. If you've begun to serve as trustee, but later decide that you don't want to be trustee anymore, you can resign. No one can be forced to be a trustee, although a resigning trustee has ongoing duties to wrap up his or her tenure.

Recognize that resigning and ending your tenure raises a whole host of issues which will not be discussed in this book. There are, however, a few points to address.

Although you can give notice of your resignation at any time you would like to, you can't just shut off your duties and responsibilities like turning off a light switch. During the resignation process, you will want to transition the trusteeship to the successor trustee. Until the trusteeship is handed over to, and accepted by, the successor trustee, you have an ongoing duty to continue to administer the trust properly. You can't just quit and throw up your hands and close your eyes. My point is: don't think it's easy-in, easy-out. You just can't ditch and bail at a moment's notice. Not only do you have a duty to the beneficiaries of the trust to get them in good hands, but from a selfish standpoint, you want to close the books in a proper and timely manner – meaning that you want to leave the trusteeship knowing that there is no lingering liability that can come back and harm you. You don't want to resign on a Monday, and hand over everything to the successor, and then get sued on a Tuesday, right? (That's what lawyers are for.)

At the point of resignation, while still serving, you should be selfish. You will want to be discharged or released for your service as trustee. In other words, you want some certainty, some recognition, that what you did as trustee was proper and that no one will come back at a later time and sue you for alleged improper acts. This is important, but beyond the scope of this book: that's what the lawyers are for.

Multiple Trustees

You may not like your co-trustees. The grantor may have appointed multiple trustees who are required to serve together.

Even if you had a cordial personal relationship with those persons in the past, a trust can change all that.

Co-trustees administer the trust by majority rule unless the trust document demands unanimous decisions. A recurring problem is when there are only two co-trustees and they do not get along – and of course are required to agree on everything. In such a case, it may make sense to have a third co-trustee such as an impartial trust attorney or bank or trust company serve as the tiebreaker. The bank can also invest and manage the assets, provide monthly statements, and assemble data for tax and other purposes.

A co-trustee may not simply rely on the work of the other co-trustee and avoid liability. Although you have a duty to cooperate with your co-trustee, you have a duty to do your own work, to use your own judgment, to form your own opinions, and to develop and act on your own, individual, thoughts. You can't simply point to the other co-trustee because they may be smarter and have more experience. You can't turn a blind eye to any aspect of the trusteeship. To the contrary, it's your job to watch and monitor your co-trustee for the benefit of your beneficiaries.

So let me dispel any misconceptions or myth that you will have a lesser, limited, or diminished role just because there is a co-trustee. Your potential liability for mismanagement is certainly not diminished. While it may make sense for the co-trustees to divvy up some of the work, and even take charge with certain tasks, each co-trustee is still required to know what's going on with the other co-trustee, and to insure that all actions are proper and in the best interests of all beneficiaries.

> The truth is that one may dispose of one's property in any manner. There is no right to an inheritance. Just about anyone can be dis-inherited.

At the risk of sounding cynical, co-trustees often don't get along. That's why they call us.

If Co-Trustees Disagree

If a co-trustee takes an action or does something which you believe is improper, you have a duty to notify the other co-trustees, and otherwise state your objection or dissent in writing. There is no uniform rule across the country as to whether stating your dissent in writing exonerates you from liability. You may need to do more. Certainly we can think of actions by co-trustees that you disagree with but do not or will not necessarily harm the trust or require you to take further action. Reasonable trustees might disagree.

Example 1: Assume that 20% of the trust's portfolio consists of one privately held company. A vote is taken by the trustees on whether to retain the stock concentration or not. A single, dissenting co-trustee does not agree to retain the concentration but is outvoted 2 to 1. The dissenting co-trustee should absolutely have his or her dissent reflected in writing and on the record. It is not unusual for co-trustees to have regular meetings and to have minutes of the meetings recorded, approved and retained. If the co-trustees are not keeping meeting minutes, record the dissent in writing (email or letter.)

Example 2: Assume that trust real estate was appraised at $2 million. A developer who employs the daughter of two co-trustees wants to purchase it for less than appraised value. Your written dissent is not enough. The sale for less than the appraised value, to a buyer which has a personal connection to the two co-trustees, requires you to take greater action. You should point out, immediately and in writing, this act of self-dealing, the conflict of interest, and seek their rationale for the sale. If your inquiry is met with deaf ears, you, as trustee, would have a duty to either enjoin the sale, or otherwise seek their removal, through court action. You might even, perhaps more simply, ask that the court appoint a temporary or special trustee to deal with just the real property.

Sense Of Entitlement

You have no right to an inheritance. So you're your parents' child. So what?

Many beneficiaries have a misplaced sense of entitlement to an inheritance. They fully expect that mom or dad will leave them property or money. The truth is that one may dispose of one's property in any manner. There is no right to an inheritance. Just about anyone can be disinherited. Further, many states, like Florida, have a very strong public policy in favor of permitting a citizen to dispose of their property at death in any manner they wish.

That means that the decedent can stand on the deck of a ship, and throw his or her money overboard or leave it all in trust for a pet—as long as they are competent and know what they are doing. One may disinherit his or her adult children by, for example, leaving everything to a neighbor or a mistress or a charity. It's their money. You can do with it as you wish.

"It's true that I inherit most of her estate. But her kids didn't come to the wedding, didn't come home for holidays, never remembered a birthday, and never called... Thank God!"

Other than dealing with a spouse, your right to dispose of your property during life and at death is virtually unfettered. There's a saying in Florida that the freedom to contract includes the freedom to make a bad bargain. Likewise, in the context of giving away your wealth, you can give it to whomever you like, and for whatever purpose you desire, and even if it may be considered foolish or stupid by others. The bottom line for trusts is this: the grantor can disinherit many people who may mistakenly believe they are going to receive an inheritance. And a trust is a perfect way to do that. The bad part, however, is that a disgruntled beneficiary may take it out on you.

The Audacity Of The Trust

The trust is family members' ball and chain around their inheritance.

While many family members have a mistaken belief that they are actually entitled to an inheritance, imagine how frustrated, even angry, they become when they learn that the decedent left them nothing – or left more money to others, or were left an inheritance in trust – with strings attached. The beneficiaries view trusts as handcuffs on their money. The trustee is the warden of the prison or jail cell whose permission must be sought for just about every dollar.

Many times beneficiaries will direct their frustration with their parent or the grantor of the trust to you, the trustee. They're upset that mom or dad did not throw money in their laps. Many trusts permit the trustee to distribute, or not distribute, trust funds (cash), in their discretion, to beneficiaries. Typically, a beneficiary may ask a trustee for money for a specific purpose. Beneficiaries hate asking the trustee for what they view as their own money. Beneficiaries hate the idea that some third-party, the trustee, gets to make the decision about whether the beneficiary receives a slice of "their" inheritance.

This setup or process makes beneficiaries feel insecure, that they can't be trusted with money. It projects beneficiaries into a businesslike arena that they are uncomfortable in, particularly because they view their inheritance as family money, something very personal to them, which should not be formal nor business – like. It removes any slice of family or personal relationship and makes the trust relationship a business requiring beneficiaries to request money from the trustee – a process which they find frustrating, time consuming, and demeaning, even akin to groveling. Beneficiaries will often seek counsel and attempt to "bust" the trust, sue you, or remove you as trustee, or get more money than they may be receiving.

Financial Ir-Responsibility

The cold hard truth: Had mom or dad thought that their child was responsible with money, they would not have placed it in trust, but rather would have given it outright – or made the beneficiary a co-trustee.

There are a number of good reasons why funds should be left in trust, even for the benefit of prudent, financially saavy, and responsible, beneficiaries. But financially saavy and responsible beneficiaries are the great exception and certainly not the rule.

Many would argue that most people are irresponsible with money, particularly large sums of inherited money, so-called "found money" – money that appears out of the blue much like a lottery winning. Although I've not read any studies on this matter, my best guess is that most people don't prudently manage their inheritance nor let it build for retirement or a rainy day, but rather they spend 90% of it within the first 24 months of inheriting it. It will be your responsibility to deal with this.

The state of Florida enjoys a strong public policy supporting its residents' right to dispose of their wealth as they see fit, including placing administrative and management restrictions on that wealth.

COURT

PROBATE DIVISION

Translation: Your Mom didn't trust you with the money, so she left it in a trust.

Trustee As Psychologist

A big part of your job will be handling, or learning how to handle, the beneficiaries, and their emotions, demands, and insecurities. Still want to be a trustee? You have to know why you want to serve.

Many beneficiaries do not like their trustee. *"Why didn't you just give me the money?"* they ask. *"Why did you leave my money in trust?"*

If a trust permits discretionary distributions of funds to beneficiaries, the beneficiary must apply for, or request, money from the trustee(s). Requesting money is an entire process, which may not be complicated nor long, but is, nonetheless, a process – with certain basic, even simple, steps which need to be followed. This often infuriates beneficiaries because they often have a false sense of entitlement.

Serving as trustee will require you to balance the person-alities of various beneficiaries. We all know that not all family members get along. Families are not immune from highly charged, deep, personal feelings, animosities, jealousies and pettiness. Let's face it, the phrase *dysfunctional family* which is being thrown around is now the normal state of affairs. Ozzie and Harriet and Ward and June Cleaver and their wonderful children don't seem to exist anymore. If they do, they all have lawyers.

TRADITIONAL FAMILY TREE

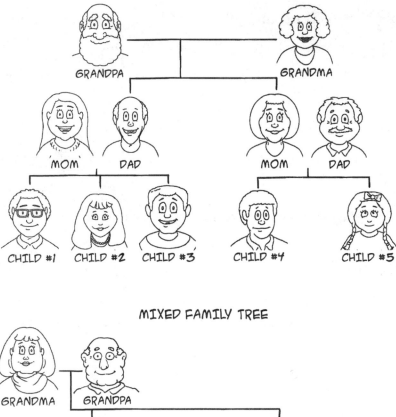

MIXED FAMILY TREE

"PALM BEACH" FAMILY TREE

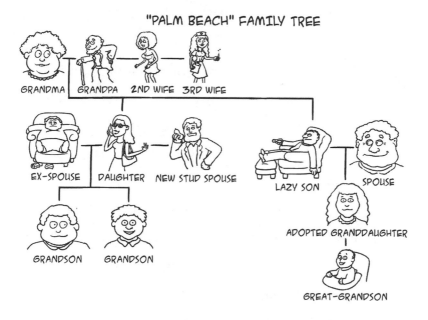

A trust takes all those family members' personal feelings and emotions, all that baggage, adds money, to create a financial stew into which the beneficiaries are thrown. When mom or dad created the trust, they may not have realized that they were linking all their beneficiaries financially. In many instances, when beneficiaries don't get along, it makes more sense to cut their financial ties by either creating multiple separate shares within the trust or creating separate trusts—one for each adult beneficiary, perhaps even with various trustees. In some instances, it may make sense to defy the grantor's intent by simply busting up the trust by giving each beneficiary an outright share now and terminating the trust. Why? Some people have such disdain for each other, it makes no sense to put them in the same financial bed.

You will be faced with the personal feelings and emotions which existed within a family which may, or may not have, surfaced or shown its ugly head – until now. Many times it takes the death of a family member, or money, to bring issues to the surface.

If one sibling was always jealous of another sibling, you are going to hear about it. If the middle child is jealous of the baby, you're going to hear how the baby got everything, and the middle child was neglected. If the oldest sibling thinks their younger brother spends too much money, or has a tramp for a wife, you will know about it. If you think I am embellishing or over embellishing, I am not. Seriously. You will hear stories of sibling rivalries, jealousies, mixed emotions and feelings of inadequacy or inattention. Childhood fights over choo-choo trains will rise to the surface once again. One probate court judge has described trust and estate litigation and disputes as being nasty as a divorce but without the sex. A trust, like a family business, can be nothing more than a financial soap opera played out in emails, angry letters and in lawyers' conference rooms. And this is only for a single family. Imagine the fun when you have multiple families.

Palm Beach Marriage

People are having multiple marriages and multiple families. The "traditional" family doesn't seem to exist anymore. Ironically the dysfunctional family is now the traditional family. While a trustee doesn't necessarily get "battle pay", a trustee gets the most action from trusts which benefit second and third spouses and children from a prior relationship.

> Marital trusts for the benefit of adult children and younger second and third spouses have become the Attorneys Full Employment Act!

Consider the typical Palm Beach marriage involving a marital trust: the well-off 70 year old male divorces his spouse, with whom he has had two children, and remarries – a thirty year old un-employed bombshell. The adult children from the grantor's first marriage are in their mid 40's and have children of their own. The adult children know that the young surviving spouse has a long life expectancy and that they won't see a dime of the marital trust, if at all, until her demise – which could be decades from now. The surviving spouse may want to live off that trust and may have no other means of income or support. The children will be angered by the surviving spouse's use of those trust funds and want to scrutinize each principal distribution which is given to her. A distant or cool relation-ship between the adult children and the surviving spouse will turn to cold, bitter feelings, which later turn to outright animosity. Imagine how the relationship only worsens when the surviving spouse takes up with a perceived ne'er-do-well, or a handsome golf pro, fisherman or trainer, as a lover, or, worse, a new spouse. Marital trusts typically provide no restriction or termination of rights if the surviv-ing spouse lives with someone, or remarries. Do you, the trustee, really want to be the referee in this type of scenario?

Are You Responsible, A Number-Cruncher, Or A Control Freak?

Some people are designated, or nominated, as trustees in the trust document or may otherwise have a natural interest in serving as trustee. You may like finance, business, legal issues, may be number-crunchers or have a back ground in finance or law or accounting. Others quite frankly are control freaks who want to manage the money and be in charge. Which one are you?

For those with an interest in serving as trustee or a desire to control the purse strings of others, you need to temper that desire to control with reality: you serve them.

Alternatives To Serving As Trustee

If you are a beneficiary who is nominated to serve as trustee, and you want to have a say in how the trust assets are invested, you may be able to do this even if you decline to serve as trustee.

Increasingly, professional trustees are asking beneficiaries about such things as investment time horizons, risk tolerance, income needs, marginal tax brackets and a host of other issues. This is intended to assist the trustee in investing trust assets properly over the long term, mindful of after-tax and after-fee returns.

As a beneficiary, you're entitled to information and accountings which can often include monthly account statements. This means that you have the opportunity to view, in depth, on a regular basis, how the trust assets are being invested. While a trust officer at a professional trust company has neither the desire nor tolerance to hear from a trust beneficiary every single day, you should know that the lines of communication should be open, helpful, informative, and professional – both ways.

My point being: today's trust law, as well as the operation of today's trust departments of professional fiduciaries, provide a mechanism for you to be involved with the trust without you taking on the responsibilities, time commitment and potential liability of serving as a trustee. You should not accept appointment as a trustee based on the belief that you want to stay involved with the trust. You, the beneficiary, already are, and you are entitled to be.

Compensation Is Not A Good Reason To Serve

If you want to serve as trustee to make some money, think again. While it's true that a trustee is entitled to reasonable compensation, along with that pay, there comes potential liability for serving as trustee. And you're probably not going to make a six-figure income as a trustee unless the trust has assets in excess of $10 million.

Still Want To Serve?

So, if I haven't talked you, the individual, out of serving as trustee, then I hope that you will consider hiring a professional bank or trust department to serve as co-trustee with you. If you don't want to resign or decline to serve, then hire trust counsel. And read on.

Steps You Learned

1. Understand why you want to serve as trustee

2. Control freaks need not apply

3. If you sincerely don't have the time or experience to serve as trustee, walk away

4. You aren't required to serve as trustee

5. Do you really want to deal with family & funds, investments and lawyers?

2

Read The Trust Document...
Plain and Simple

You need to read, and understand, the trust document.

Welcome!

So, you have decided to serve.

Unlike years ago, today, trusts are not just for the wealthy, and the trust world is not limited to lush offices in big city banks and law firms. Trusts are now used by young and old, rich and, well, less-rich, for a variety of reasons, and to accomplish any one of dozens of objectives. These objectives may be very short-term, such as a trust to hold cash and an insurance policy until a minor child attains majority. Other trusts have long term objectives, such as creating a multi-generational trust to compound and grow over a hundred of years for the benefit of your grandchildren and more remote descendants.

This is serious stuff. Trusts come in all shapes and sizes, with varying purposes. In all cases, however, a trust is set up for the administration and management of property according to certain guidelines and confines, which are found in the trust document and local law.

The job of a trustee is to carry out the intent of the grantor, as expressed in the trust document, and according to the law which governs the trust and its administration. How do we understand the intent of the grantor? By reading the trust document. Many, many trusts are administered years after the death of the grantor, and under circumstances where the trustee never met the grantor, let alone talked to the grantor about his or her intent.

This is going to sound silly. Perhaps even obvious. But here goes: *Reading* the entire trust document is an essential prerequisite in considering whether to serve as a trustee, as well as a requirement for your tenure. Just as a restaurant operator needs to start with the menu before designing the infrastructure or running the place, so, too, must the trustee begin with the operative document: the trust agreement.

The trust may have additional documents, such as amendments, which must also be read thoroughly. *Under-*

standing the trust is another thing. If you don't understand what you are reading, or understand how a trust is to be administered, you are going to fail. The good news is that you can hire trust counsel and other advisers to assist you. The bad news is the reality that "running" a trust is a whole heck of a lot more than merely investing. If you have "run" your own money for years, and follow the markets, and read the Wall Street Journal daily, I have news for you: that isn't even close to being prepared for administering a trust.

When reading the trust document, and trying to understand how the trust is to be administered, start with the basics:

- "Who" gets "what"?
- Who are the permissible beneficiaries over what period of time?
- Who **must** you distribute income or principal to?
- Who **may** you distribute income or principal to and for what reasons?
- How much **discretion** has the grantor given to you as trustee?

Example 1:

During the lifetime of my surviving spouse, the trustee shall distribute all income to my surviving spouse at least annually. In addition, the trustee may distribute principal for the surviving spouse's health, educational maintenance, and support.

Issue: Now, consider a scenario where the surviving spouse has requested $50,000 from the trust for the purchase of a luxury automobile. Should you, as trustee, distribute $50,000 so that the surviving spouse may purchase a luxury automobile?

Answer: Not such a clear one. The challenge for the trustee is to determine whether a $50,000 luxury automobile is an appropriate distribution for the surviving spouse's health, education, maintenance or support.

Here's the challenge: At first blush, it would appear that such a distribution would not be permissible under the standards of health or education. But consider this: what if the surviving spouse told you, as trustee, that she had to drive to a chiropractor once a week, to a massage therapist twice a week, and to a doctor's office every other week, and that she needed a new vehicle to get her there safely and securely. Would this justify a $50,000 distribution from the trust for the purchase of a luxury automobile for the "health" of the surviving spouse?

"$10,000 a month? That's not enough for a good mani and pedi these days."

Example 2:

Now, consider that further down in the trust document, the following trust language appeared:

> *In deciding whether to distribute or not distribute principal to or for the benefit of my surviving spouse, the trustee shall maintain my surviving spouse in the lifestyle and*

manner in which she has become accustomed and which we enjoyed.

Same Issue/Answer: You must determine whether a $50,000 luxury automobile was something intended, or contemplated, by the standards of "maintenance" or "support".

In determining whether to grant or disapprove the surviving spouse's request for $50,000, would it help to know that the grantor and the surviving spouse always drove a luxury vehicle? Or that they only drove pre-owned, inexpensive domestic automobiles?

> The trustee needs to be guided by the grantor's intent, and certainly not the trustee's personal feelings, opinions, or attitudes—especially not the trustee's biases and emotions

Be Objective: Your Feelings Don't Matter

In reading, and understanding, the trust terms, the trustee needs to be guided by the *grantor's intent*, and certainly not the trustee's personal feelings, opinions, or attitudes.

In our example, it does not matter whether the trustee has never, personally, owned a $50,000 luxury automobile, or whether the trustee would not spend $50,000 of the trustee's own money for a luxury automobile. Rather, the sole focus for the trustee is: would the grantor want the surviving spouse to have a $50,000 luxury automobile? The trustee needs to exercise sound judgment. Your trouble begins when you insert your personal feelings or beliefs in place of objective analysis.

But the truth of the matter is, that time and time again, we revert to the trust document itself to see if it addresses issues which arise during the course of administration. Read it. Understand it. Re-read it. If you don't understand it, hire a seasoned trust attorney.

Even non-trust attorneys seek the assistance of an experienced trust attorney. Trustees are permitted to retain an attorney, which may act as trust counsel and advise the trustee on all issues regarding the trust. The trustee is entitled to compensate trust counsel a reasonable amount from the assets of the trust. The trustee is not required to pay trust counsel from the trustee's own pocket or from personal funds.

A trustee must follow the terms of the trust *in good faith*, and in a reasonable manner – at all times in an effort to effectuate the grantor's intent for the benefit of the beneficiaries.

Ignorance is no defense to wrongful or neglectful acts by a trustee. Failure to read a trust or to understand its terms, is no excuse. If you are questioned about your actions or inactions, your failure to read the trust terms or to understand them will not get you off the hook, but will probably get you removed as trustee.

While failure to read a trust or to understand its terms is not excusable, failure in the application of the trust terms is likewise wrongful. Trustees are not only required to read and comprehend and understand the terms of the trust, but they are also required – indeed they promise – to carry out the terms of the trust.

The trustee should carry out the terms of the trust in a reason able manner. Knee-jerk reaction or lightning speed are not expected, but neither is unreasonable delay. No feet dragging. When the trust's language is clear and unambiguous, there is little or no excuse for failing to comply with those terms within a reasonable time frame. What's a reasonable time frame? Use common sense. It should not take you a week to get a copy of the trust document or an investment statement to a beneficiary who requests that information. But a beneficiary should understand that a request for information on a Friday at 4:00 pm might not be responded to until the following Monday or Tuesday.

Example 3:

Grandmother takes over as the trustee of a trust which holds marketable securities and a condominium for her Daughter. Grandmother correctly re-titles the securities in the name of the trust and invests them. However, she refuses to transfer the condo to Daughter, which the trust document clearly requires. To the contrary, Grandmother permits her brother to use the condominium from time to time and does not distribute the condo to her daughter, not due to any administrative issue, but rather because they have grown estranged over the recent past. Grandmother, as trustee, does not inform Daughter of the existence of the trust nor does she provide her with copy of the trust until Daughter's attorney reads a copy of the trust.

Issue: Is there trustee liability for Grandmother?

Answer: Yes. The trustee's failure to distribute the condo to Daughter is a willful violation of the clear language of the trust. It is a breach of her fiduciary duty in the most simple of terms. It is grounds for her immediate removal as trustee and will likely subject her to a civil lawsuit and damages, which in the trust context may sometimes be referred to as a *surcharge,* or a fine against a trustee.

This condo example may seem basic, or a "no-brainer", but it happens all the time. This happened because of the poor personal relationship, or bad feelings, between Grandmother and Daughter.

Compare this latest condominium example to the prior example of a discretionary distribution request for a $50,000 luxury automobile. In the condominium example, the trustee was being vindictive and unreasonable, in clear violation of the plain language of the trust document. A bad trustee. She was supposed to distribute the condo and she purposely – intentionally – failed to do so. That's a clear cut case of the trustee breaching her fiduciary duty. But when a trustee attempts to follow the trust document in good faith, by, for example, considering a discretionary distribution request, for, say, a car, a trustee's potential liability is slightly different.

A trustee will not necessarily be subject to surcharge or damages if their analysis of the discretionary distribution request was analytical, reasonable, and in line with the grantor's intent as expressed in the language of the trust. In other words, if the trustee denied the request for $50,000 for a luxury automobile based upon a reasoned analysis, and not out of spite, vindictiveness or disharmony with the beneficiary, there is no liability. There's a difference between a *bad trustee* and one who might be viewed as a *poor trustee*.

You May Be Over-Ruled As A Trustee

In the discretionary distribution request example, even though the language of the trust is plain or straightforward, it is open to interpretation as to whether a $50,000 automobile constitutes a request for support or maintenance, and if so, whether such a distribution is proper. Reasonable minds might differ and exercise discretion differently.

When a beneficiary is not pleased with a decision of a trustee, that beneficiary may seek intervention of a court to over-rule the trustee. In the case of a discretionary distribution, the beneficiary needs to demonstrate to the court that the trustee was unreasonable or that it abused its discretion. If the trustee read the trust document, understood it, and objectively made its decision, in good faith, there is no liability. The trustee would not be subject to surcharge or damages, even if the court would overrule the trustee and order the distribution, as long as the court is convinced (finds) that the trustee's denial of the request was made in good faith and was not an abuse of discretion.

A court may have to intervene if the trust language is too ambiguous or when a provision may not make sense.

Example 3a:

A trust reads "...*upon my death, my Mercedes Benz will go to my son...*"

Issue: In actuality, the grantor has two Mercedes.

Answer: In that circumstance, on the face of the trust it is not obvious that the grantor owned two Mercedes. You or a beneficiary later learn of the two cars, and thereafter bring it to the attention of the court, if the trustee and the beneficiaries cannot resolve the issue among themselves.

Construction Actions

When reading the trust document, if the trustee is unclear what the document says or what the grantor intended, the trustee may ask a court to interpret it. Initially, the court will read the trust document and hear argument from counsel. If the court believes that the document is un-ambiguous, that is, clear on its face, then the court will simply read and construe the trust. That is why these actions are referred to as "construction" actions. They actually have nothing to do with buildings, real estate or development. If the court believes that trust language is ambiguous, or not clear on its face, then the court will receive testimony and evidence to ascertain the true intent of the grantor.

> Don't be misled by trust language which is seemingly broad, simple or "clear". The trust terms may not mean what you think they mean.

One final note about reading and understanding the trust document: not every aspect of trust law or guideline for prudent administration will be enunciated in the trust document. Don't be misled by trust language which is seemingly broad, simple or "clear". The trust terms may not mean what you think they mean when you read them.

Example 4:

The trustee shall have absolute and unfettered discretion to invest or reinvest the trust property as it sees fit from time to time, including the selection of any and all investments.

Issue: Does the trust language really give the trustee carte blanche?

Answer: No! At first blush, this trust language appears clear, unambiguous and straight to the point. It appears that the trustee has absolute free rein on investing, including the important topic of which assets, and asset classes, to choose. Wrong!

What this trust language does not tell you is that a trustee must be prudent, must have an investment plan or strategy which requires a careful and thoughtful consideration and analysis of many factors, including:

- What asset classes to invest in
- When to invest
- How much to invest
- When to sell or exit a particular investment

This trust language can be misleading or provide false sense of comfort to a trustee. An individual trustee, and certainly one who is inexperienced, may mistakenly believe that such language would permit the trustee to invest entirely in, for example, fixed income instruments such as bonds. Or, a trustee may improperly believe that the trust would permit the trustee to retain a single piece of real estate in trust, and no other assets.

This trust language would not provide a defense to a trustee who retains a non-income-producing piece of real property which comprises, for example, all of the trust's value – without having a prudent strategy or plan which explains either why that real property is being retained or when and under what circumstances it is expected to be sold.

When it comes to investing, particularly in today's litigious society, and particularly with certain recent court rulings across the country, broad or seemingly protective investing language in the trust document, including language which attempts to exonerate, or hold a trustee harmless, provides little comfort to trust counsel. It seems everyone knows that a trustee needs to be a "prudent" investor. Few non trust professionals fully understand what that means or how it is applied. Few actually know exactly what that means or how to invest others' funds. Don't assume a plain reading of the trust document permits you to invest without a specific plan for each and every asset and asset class, let alone haphazardly or inattentively.

You need to read, re-read, and understand the trust document: even when it seems clear.

Steps You Learned

1. Read, and re-read, the trust document – it's your bible

2. It's your job to understand what the trust document says, and what it means under local trust law – each day and all the time

3. If you are struggling with understanding the document, hire trust counsel

4. Adhere to the trust terms in good faith – don't be cute, don't ignore them and don't self-deal

5. Don't assume there is only one interpretation to the trust document: even "clear" language has two sides to it.

6. What you may think the trust terms mean could be dead wrong

Retain Trust Counsel

Help…you'll need it.

So now that you have decided that you want to be a trustee, now that you understand *why* you want to serve, and now that you have read the trust document completely, we can move on to the finer details of beginning to administer the trust for the benefit of the beneficiaries.

Administering a trust means that it's your job to:

- protect the beneficiaries and the trust property
- safeguard that property
- invest it prudently so that it hopefully increases in value over time

- monitor the assets in light of the decisions which you've made
- watch costs and expenses
- share all this information with those who you have chosen to serve, namely, the beneficiaries.

But along the way, you, like any legal actor, should also use the law to protect yourself. While it is certainly true that you must serve your beneficiaries, and that you must be loyal to them, nothing prohibits you from taking advantage of safeguards which the law provides trustees. It is only common sense to do so. After all, you are agreeing to serve as trustee, not indemnify the beneficiaries from every market downturn or bump along the road.

One of the best ways to both assist you with administering the trust for the beneficiaries, and to protect yourself as trustee, is to retain experienced trust counsel to advise you.

Don't Go It Alone: It Is Expected That You Will Have Trust Counsel

It is not only acceptable for a trustee to hire a trust lawyer, but it is expected. Most states have statues which specifically permit the trustee to retain experts and professionals including attorneys and accountants. Likewise, most trust documents say the same thing.

Don't feel that hiring trust counsel will make you look weak, or suggest any wrong doing to beneficiaries or a judge. Even the most seasoned individual trustees have counsel. Many Americans prepare their own tax returns, on their own, when they shouldn't – they should have an accountant prepare them. Hiring trust counsel is not a big deal.

Some individuals may believe that hiring an attorney "sends the wrong message" to the beneficiaries. Let's face it: hiring an attorney most times sends a serious message to the other side. This may be doubly true in the case of a trust where one is dealing with family members and money. Many may believe that you've done something wrong (why hire an attorney if you've done everything correctly?).

My suggestion is to disclose the hiring of trust counsel and to simply be upfront with the beneficiaries: explain that the trust law, and the trust document, both contemplate a trustee hiring trust counsel for the limited role of advising the trustee on trust law and administration. You might even say that the hiring of trust counsel should not be interpreted in any other manner and that you will monitor the fees paid to counsel from trust assets.

When I was a boy growing up north of Boston, just after attorneys were permitted to begin advertising on television, a local attorney had a TV ad with a saying that summed it up perfectly: *"Don't go it alone."* Although he was a personal injury attorney, trustees should heed his advice.

Dispelling Common Myths – Money Changes Everything

Many believe that their family, their loved ones, would never sue them. Let me dispel this myth. 9 out of 10 calls to our firm are from a prospective client distraught over what a family member did…and ready to sue them. When you put money in the mix, rules change. Love changes. The sense of family changes.

Let's face it, many times it may not even be your immediate family member, but rather the in-law or dominating, know-it-all spouse of your relative who has no interest in the trust, that is complaining the loudest. Or threatening the most. I have repeatedly found that it is often the spouse or boyfriend or girlfriend – who has no money or interest in the underlying disagreement or dispute – who is the catalyst. The agitator. A word of caution to trustees: don't believe a self-imposed myth that your family members won't sue you, or seek your removal as trustee. They do it every day and hire lawyers like me to get it done.

Hiring trust counsel and actually hearing – objectively – what they have to say may just open your eyes, your ears and your mind. That's because once you hire counsel, they can assist you in dispelling two other common myths: that you don't need counsel and that what you are doing could never be questioned.

Dispelling Myths – Why Do I Need You? I'm Not Doing Anything Wrong.

My suggestion is to at least retain counsel when your trusteeship begins. If you find that you don't need legal advice you can discharge the attorney. But it would be wrong for trustees to work in a vacuum and not have the benefit of counsel.

Example:

Recently, I was called by a CPA whose trustee client was dissatisfied with his present trust attorney and wanted a more "aggressive" attorney. When we started discussing the facts, it was clear that the trustee did not like the advice he was receiving from his attorney. He didn't even think he needed one!

Issue: The trustee thought his lawyer was wrong for raising issues which the trustee believed were not issues; and for making suggestions which the trustee didn't like.

Answer: The trustee didn't necessarily want more of a fighter. What he wanted was advice which matched his own personal beliefs. The trustee was also a beneficiary of a trust which had one asset: very valuable income producing real property. The trustee was the sole income beneficiary! The other, remainder, beneficiaries, and their counsel, asked the trustee to sell the real estate and diversify the investments. Sounds reasonable, right? After all, why put all your trust "eggs" in one "basket"? And isn't diversification a very basic tenet of prudent investing?

The trustee was fighting that notion and was worried that if he sold the property, his income would decrease. The trustee also had this personal affinity for the real property in the trust. He loved that asset and he loved "working it." He didn't want to sell it because, personally, it gave him something to do. I advised that, first of all, that analysis was not proper because he was placing his own, personal interests above those whom he agreed to serve (the beneficiaries) and his ongoing duty to prudently invest the trust assets. This included avoiding asset concentrations and also diversifying the trust property.

I told him that if he wanted to simply be assured that he would receive the same income if he sold the real estate, that I could assist him, because there were methods in the trust law which provided opportunities to do this. The trustee hemmed and hawed. Then he asked me what I thought of not selling the real estate but rather exchanging it in a tax-free manner for another piece of real property.

He just didn't get it. But I did. The trustee enjoyed managing the real property. He liked real estate as an investment. He didn't like stocks and bonds or administering a portfolio of equities. He liked being in control.

Well, I advised him that the advice he was getting from his present attorney was good advice, and that there was no reason to hire me. I also advised him that he didn't even realize that what he was doing, indeed his analysis, was wrong. I started to explain to him what the "prudent investor" rule was, and what his duties as a trustee were.

"I know that!" he interrupted.

My reply: "No.... Clearly, I don't think you do."

I felt like Jerry Seinfeld in that episode when he made a car rental reservation but there's no car at the rental company when he goes to pick it up, even though they acknowledge Jerry's reservation. Seinfeld starts explaining that he needs a car and that he made a reservation. The rental car employee interrupts Seinfeld and tells him in a condescending manner that she knows what a reservation is. Seinfeld deadpans: "No, I don't think you do."

*"I thought dental and electric bills
were 'health' and 'maintenance.'"*

I felt the same frustration. I just wasn't getting through to
this prospective client and trustee. He was in denial and
embracing, indeed holding on to, two common myths: he
didn't need trust counsel and what he was doing was right.
He just didn't get it. And I didn't get the business.

Moral of the story: you may not realize that what you are doing is wrong. In fact, he stated that under his trusteeship the value of the real estate went up dramatically, to which I replied: *"That's what you are supposed to do."* Second moral of the story: you probably should do more than merely hear what your attorney has to say: you should listen. And if you don't believe in or trust your attorney: you should fire that attorney.

Your Downside As Trustee: Damages And Surcharge

Let's get selfish for a moment. You need an attorney to protect you. There is nothing wrong with you or any other legal actor for that matter trying to limit liability and to protect yourself from unnecessary or harmful lawsuits.

Administering a trust is, in some ways, like running a small business and it's OK to get assistance. We live in a litigious society. And trust beneficiaries tend to be very litigious.

If you are found to have done something wrong as trustee, if you violated your duties, there is real liability, or potential liability to you, which is personal. This means that if you are found to have done something wrong by a judge, the damages which you may be ordered to pay will not come from the trust, but from your own personal funds: your checking account or savings account. Don't have enough? You'll have to sell some of your investments or assets.

And doing something wrong, or violating your duties, is not restricted to egregious acts of stealing or improper use of trust funds. You may be responsible for damages if you are simply not doing a good job and you should have done better. As this chapter is trying to suggest, many times individual trustees don't even know they are doing anything wrong!

If a trustee is found liable for damages, you may be required to pay damages, reimburse the other side their costs or expenses, and even pay attorneys fees to the "winning" side. You may be surcharged or fined for your improper actions. If you used trust funds to pay your attorney, you may be ordered to reimburse the trust for those funds and in essence pay all that money back.

Still Think You Don't Need A Lawyer?!

You May Be Prohibited From Using Trust Funds To Defend Yourself

If you act improperly, the other side may seek to prohibit you from using trust funds to pay your attorneys if there is a lawsuit. This is an important exception to the general rule which permits a trustee to hire counsel and pay from trust assets. Although many states have a rule or statute which sets out a procedure for this, it is typically limited to situations which involve some conflict of interest by the trustee or act of self-dealing. This issue would when there is a pending lawsuit and the trustee faces individual liability.

Hiring Trust Counsel

Although a trustee may hire or retain trust counsel, do so wisely. A trustee cannot frivolously hire help when it is not needed. The law works in this manner to not hinder you from reaching out for help; to assist you in obtaining good advisors to assist your administration. Counsel should be retained only when needed and not necessarily for each and every minute of trustee work. After all, you are the trustee and while a good attorney can guide you, you have to do the work. You can't delegate to trust counsel any discretion or decision-making: that's your job. Discretion is rarely, if ever, permitted to be delegated by a trustee. That means that you have to make the tough calls. The role of your attorney is to advise and guide. In the end, you can listen to or ignore her advice.

Starting Your Tenure

Retain counsel when you begin your trusteeship. There are unique issues which a new or incoming trustee faces which you won't know about, but which experienced trust counsel will.

- Do you have a duty to investigate the acts of the prior trustee?

- Should you sue the prior trustee?

- Do you know how to gather all the trust assets or even how or where to look for them?

- How and when do you communicate with the beneficiaries?

- Should I retain or fire any service providers?

Trust counsel, from the outset, can assist you with these issues and help you provide the proper notices to beneficiaries – even when beneficiaries know who you are and that you are coming on board as trustee.

Do Your Own Work: It's Your Fault, Not Mine

Don't assume that what the prior trustee did in the past was proper or appropriate. Far too many times, we hear from trustees that they are merely following what the prior trustee did. Too many times we are hearing that the present trustee is assuming that what the prior trustee did was OK. One word of advice: don't!

You have a duty to investigate the acts of the prior trustee.

- What assets are there

- What transpired

- Independently evaluate the trust, the actions of the prior trustee

- Chart a course, or create a plan or strategy for administration and investment

- Make your own independent evaluation and decisions, particularly if the prior trustee did something bad, or harmful to the trust.

> Don't fall asleep behind the wheel.
> You, and only you, are driving.

Likewise, don't retain the trust investments which the prior trustee had simply because you believe the prior trustee knew what he or she was doing. You have a duty to review the assets yourself and retain, sell or purchase as *you believe* is prudent – not as the prior trustee may have believed. Simply following in the footsteps of a predecessor trustee is no excuse for wrongdoings and no replacement for your own independent analysis, prudence and judgment. Remember that you need to exercise independent judgment and sound discretion.

Ideally, you should consult with counsel even **before** you accept the trusteeship, although you may have to pay for that advice on your own dime.

You should retain counsel with some experience in the area of trust administration including advising trustees. Hiring an experienced trust attorney is ideal. You may compensate them a reasonable amount, which often depends on where you are located, the complexity of the issues you are faced with, based upon an hourly rate and the amount of time required to provide legal services. If you are in a mid-sized city in the south, the hourly rates for trust attorneys with 20 years' of experience may be $300-$600. It is probably substantially higher in the largest metropolitan areas and considerably lower for those with less experience, or in smaller legal markets. You can't pay a new attorney at the rate of a senior partner. You shouldn't pay a lawyer with no trust experience the same rate as one with substantial experience. You shouldn't hire your spouse, relative or best friend.

Remember: you are under a microscope. Everything which you do will be scrutinized, examined and, if wrong, corrected – either voluntarily by you, or maybe by a judge.

Attorney Client Privilege

The information, research, and communications regarding the trust which are shared by and between you and your trust counsel may be protected from disclosure to third parties including beneficiaries. Said another way, communications, emails, conferences, letters which you have with your attorney can't be discovered by anyone else. Your communications with your counsel are privileged and need not be shared with anyone. This protection provides you with the safety and encouragement to speak freely with your attorney without fear that it will be later disseminated to or discovered by somebody that may be adverse to you, such as disgruntled beneficiary.

Please note however that not all jurisdictions may take this approach. Whenever you hire trust counsel, an important point which should be discussed is whether communications are indeed protected. Some jurisdictions take the position that your beneficiaries may indeed be able to obtain the thoughts, ideas and strategies and feelings which you shared with your attorney.

Relevant Information

Your trust counsel can also assist you with your duty to provide relevant information and accountings to all beneficiaries. You will be required to disclose to your beneficiaries all actions which you've taken as trustee. Any purposeful or intentional nondisclosure of material facts, or any partial disclosure, or half-truths, are acts of fraud. Not only are you required to disclose what the trust assets are, what "buys" and "sells" you made of marketable securities, but also such things as expenses you've incurred on behalf of the trust including what you paid to your attorneys. Yes, this means that all beneficiaries will know what you are paying your attorneys from trust funds. So, scrutinize those invoices carefully. After all, that's your job. The beneficiaries are entitled to know what you're spending their money on.

Protecting Your Hide

In certain states, such as Florida, if you disclose certain information and provide what's called a "limitations notice", then a beneficiary is limited to six months to sue you. Although this certainly won't get you excited, in the legal world, this is fantastic. Put another way: if you properly disclose certain information in writing and also inform the beneficiary that they only have a limited time to object to anything which you have disclosed, then this may create a very short (e.g. six month) statute of limitations.

This is an amazing and incredible safeguard for trustees. Most statutes of limitations are for four to five years. Your trust counsel should be familiar with the statutes of limitations and with any protections and safeguards which the governing law provides you as trustee, to limit your liability.

One final note: this short statute of limitations only applies to matters which are adequately and completely disclosed. You can't hide the ball or attempt to mislead. Just come out and say it. Disclose. If you spent $50,000 on attorneys fees or for an accounting, then your disclosure document should say that. Don't disguise the $50,000 expenditure as some nondescript matter.

There is a recurring and general rule for trustees: disclose, disclose, disclose!

Your trust disclosure documents and accounting should be clear and concise, easily understandable, and in plain English. Don't use accounting terms, legalese or other terms which the average person or layperson does not understand. Put it in a letter and get it to the beneficiaries in the manner required by local law. Don't use a small font: use at least 12 point font.

If there's a close call on whether something you disclose to a beneficiary was clear or not, or adequately disclosed, or confusing, a court is going to side with the beneficiary and rule that what you disclosed was not adequately disclosed – meaning no six month statute of limitations.

Remember: your attorney is not the trustee. You are. At the beginning of any trust relationship or the beginning of your tenure as trustee, it's understandable that there may be some degree of upfront work. That should taper off after time. You will certainly need to meet with your counsel at least annually to discuss the prior year, disclosing relevant information and to prepare accountings.

You may also speak to counsel more frequently if you are involved in more important or other, major, transactions which your counsel is assisting you with.

Who Pays For Trust Counsel?

Other than receiving reasonable compensation, the trustee should not use trust funds for a personal benefit. You can't have trust counsel perform personal services for you, and pay for those services from trust funds.

It is recommended that any attorney you hire for the trust, clearly distinguishes work on behalf of the trust from any ser vices which the lawyer may provide to you on an individual, personal basis. Ideally, your trust counsel should only represent you in your capacity as trustee and you should have a separate lawyer, separate law firm, handling your personal matters. The trustee may not use trust funds to pay an attorney to prepare his will, or to review a contract or a prenuptial agreement. This is true no matter how little the cost of legal services may be, regardless of whether the attorney provides a discount to the trustee, or how good a job the trustee is doing. Personal expenses are personal expenses. You pay for them – not the trust. No exceptions. There is no "gray" here: it's black and white. If you don't know if an expense or cost is personal or if it benefits the trust, then it's personal. You pay for it out of your own pocket.

Steps You Learned

1. Hire a pro

2. Don't be naïve to think you can administer the trust without assistance

3. Don't think for a minute that a family member won't sue you

4. Being a trustee is a lot more than just buying stocks

5. Let your trust counsel assist with complying with trust law, and protecting your hide from potential liability

They Have a Right to Know

You must notify all beneficiaries of the existence of the trust, your contact information and beneficiaries' rights to obtain relevant information about the trust and its administration.

This may seem obvious to many, but I assure you that it's not to a few: you actually have to tell your beneficiaries about the existence of the trust and your identity.

I can't tell you how many times beneficiaries have told me that they didn't know someone had created a trust for them, or that they were a beneficiary. Many times, beneficiaries are not even sure who the trustee is.

Quite often, trusts are created without notice to the successor trustee or the future beneficiaries. The first time anyone even knows of the existence of the trust is after the grantor passes away. This is understandable in certain instances.

Consider one's revocable trust which is fully revocable or "change-able" during the grantor's life. Once the trust becomes irrevocable, such as upon the death of the grantor, the successor trustee has a duty to notify all beneficiaries who probably didn't know they were a beneficiary until now.

This is accomplished by writing a simple letter and sending it via US Mail. Increasingly, email is used. The notice of trust will inform each beneficiary of:

- The name of the trust
- The identity of the trustee
- The address or contact information for the trustee and who counsel is
- Perhaps a statement akin to a beneficiaries' "Bill of Rights"
- The right to receive a complete copy of the trust agreement, including all amendments
- Relevant information regarding the trust and its administration
- Other information required to be disclosed under the law which governs the administration of the trust.

In addition to a written notice that may be provided by communicating directly with the beneficiaries, the trustee may also be required to file a more public or formal notice of trust. A successor trustee of a decedent's revocable trust, which is now irrevocable when the grantor passes away, may be required to file a notice in any probate proceeding pertaining to the estate of the decedent grantor, or in the county records for the county where the decedent passed away.

This court-filed or public records-filed notice of trust is in tended to identify the trustee and discloses the existence of the trust. It also gives notice to creditors and recognizes that a decedent's revocable trust may be responsible for the payment of the decedent's debts and obligations.

Beneficiaries of a grantor's revocable trust should understand that the assets which comprise a revocable trust must first be used to satisfy all obligations of the decedent – before those assets may benefit the beneficiaries.

Example: the decedent dies with a revocable trust containing $10 million in marketable securities and cash. The trust states that after the death of decedent it shall be administered for his surviving spouse and children. The grantor's trust is liable for all of the decedent's debts, expenses, and obligations which may not be satisfied by his other assets. If the decedent had a $1 million bank account which was in his own, individual, name, and $4 million in loans, debts, and expenses of administration, the trust would be funded only with $7 million. One may not place assets in trust during life, and then keep those assets free from creditors. You can't shun your known creditors by placing assets in a trust for the benefit of your loved ones.

A notice of trust may also limit the time frame for someone to challenge, or attack, the validity of the trust. The governing law might provide that a notice shall indicate that if anyone wants to challenge the validity, that they only have a matter of time to do so. This is often important when a trustee, or one's lawyers, know that a disgruntled family member, perhaps not receiving an expected inheritance, is expected to litigate.

*"I'm the trustee now. Crystal, his former trainer,
said I should have done this years ago."*

Asset Protection

Asset protection is the legitimate use of legal strategies and techniques to safeguard assets and property from some future or unknown attack. Asset protection strategies must at all times be legal and ethical. Asset protection strategies do not include hindering or thwarting your known and existing creditors. Some very simple asset protection strategies may be available to you simply by taking advantage of certain statutes in your jurisdiction. For example, annuities, IRAs, retirement plans, joint accounts may be protected. There is most likely a *spendthrift provision* in your trust document which protects trust assets from creditors of the beneficiaries. A spendthrift provision typically instructs the trustee that the trustee may not use trust funds to pay a debt or obligation of the beneficiary. If anyone makes a demand upon you as trustee to pay a purported debt or loan or obligation of a trust beneficiary, immediately contact trust counsel. Don't simply pay the debt believing that you are being responsive. Read the trust terms and obtain information to understand the debt or loan or obligation.

Steps You Learned

1. One of your basic duties as a trustee is to let the beneficiaries know of the existence of the trust

2. Introduce yourself: even if you are already known to your beneficiaries

3. Confirm that your beneficiaries have rights

4. Provide your contact information

5. Your trust attorney can do this for you

5

Your Duty To Inform & Account

*You must inform the beneficiaries of all important events
and matters, and keep detailed, straightforward records.*

A trustee has a present (right now!) and ongoing duty to provide relevant information about the trust, and a trustee's actions, to each of the beneficiaries. This also includes a duty to account, on a regular basis, and to otherwise show the beneficiaries the trust's "books."

Duties of a trustee are fiduciary duties. These duties are among the most serious, most important and highest duties found in the law. The law and your beneficiaries impose great trust and confidence in you. As such, the law subjects your actions and your conduct to the closest scrutiny. If you believe that such close scrutiny is any way unfair or unnecessary, then being a trustee is not for you. In that case, you should not accept a trusteeship, and if you are currently serving as trustee, you should resign.

Many view a trustee's role as merely, or, more or less limited to, purchasing and selling stocks and bonds. But in actuality, a trustee's role is considerably greater and more encompassing than just prudent investing. Managing money, determining what asset classes to have in a trust's portfolio, is merely one part of the responsibilities of serving as trustee. One of the most important duties that a trustee has is to provide relevant information to each of the beneficiaries. The beneficiaries have an absolute right to know exactly and everything that is going on in their trust. It is your responsibility, and duty, as trustee, to keep them apprised of all aspects of trust administration.

What Is Relevant Information?

Relevant information has been described as any so-called reasonable or everyday information which one would expect or want to know about the trust, its assets, and its administration.

A more cynical view would define relevant information to include all information about the trust, specifically including any information which the trustee doesn't want to share with the beneficiaries, or which he thinks the beneficiaries do not need to know. After all, as the saying goes, if you have to wonder whether you need to disclose that information, you better disclose.

In general, the trustee is required to disclose:

- The identity and location of all assets

- Fair market value of all assets as of a particular time, perhaps the carrying value or the cost basis or purchase price of the assets

- Expenditures, including disbursements for costs and expenses, including money paid for trustee compensation and trust attorneys, and other advisors

- Value of all trust funds distributed to each beneficiary including the identity of each asset distributed

- Transactions and occurrences, including income and gains and losses

The duty to disclose relevant information is very closely linked to a trustee's duty to provide accountings on a regular basis. But they are slightly different. Both duties are ongoing, but the duty to account is considered more periodic. The duty to provide an accounting is intended to give the beneficiaries a regular "snapshot" of the trust's books on a regular basis. So, typically annually, you provide each beneficiary with an accounting, in essence, a more or less formal QuickBooks spreadsheet of all the ins and outs of the trust's money. With proper tracking, and financial software, you or a bookkeeper can easily maintain the data which needs to be reflected in the accounting. Each jurisdiction has different rules on when accountings must be filed, how often they must be filed, exactly what data must be provided, and whether or not they need to be filed with a court of law.

The duty to provide relevant information is also ongoing, but is typically satisfied as the inquiry or need arises. A simple ex ample would be if a beneficiary calls, or sends an email, inquiring about the lease terms of a piece of real property which the trust owns. Conceivably the answer to the beneficiary's inquiry might be revealed on an annual accounting which would be produced next year. But why make the beneficiary wait? Well, candidly, there is no need to make the beneficiary wait.

"I want to thank the person who made this all possible... my trust attorney."

You, as trustee, should be responsive to such basic and sensible inquiries, and you clearly have a duty to disclose such information. It would be unreasonable and in bad faith to make a beneficiary wait months for a simple answer that can be provided right now. If a trust owns real property which is rented, why not provide the terms and conditions and a copy of the lease? You could make this information available by way of a trust disclosure document which we discussed in the last chapter.

Trust Disclosure Document

How much information does a trustee need to disclose to each beneficiary and how much time does a trustee need to spend attending to beneficiary inquiries?

Example:

In a typical disclosure document, the trustee might disclose:

- a $5 million account at the ABC Brokerage Company as of a particular date, enclosing a monthly statement
- $3000 is distributed to the trustee each month in the form of trustee compensation for ordinary services
- $5,000 was paid to trust counsel in the last month
- a piece of real property located at 123 Main St., Any-town, USA was distributed to beneficiary John Smith pursuant to Article V of the trust document
- $10,000 cash per month has been distributed to the surviving spouse
- $30,000 was used to pay the annual premium for a life insurance policy owned by the trust
- Any potential or pending litigation

Increasingly, trustees are sending a cover letter to beneficiaries and highlighting important or major transactions or occurrences during a particular period of time, and otherwise explaining entries on an accompanying statement which might not at first glance be completely understood or clear. Following this cover letter, trustees are attaching monthly statements for the financial account where trust assets may be held. In this sense, beneficiaries are receiving *informal accountings* on a monthly basis. Other relevant information may be disclosed or even attached, such as a real estate tax bill, a listing agreement or purchase and sale agreement, a lease, a schedule of rental payments received.

A trustee must be responsive in a reasonable and timely manner. This means that you do not necessarily need to return a beneficiary's phone call that day or within 24 hours but you do need to return the call. You need to answer questions which the beneficiaries may have and provide them with complete and satisfactory answers, although trustees are not necessarily expected to spend an entire day on the phone with the beneficiary.

You will no doubt encounter beneficiaries who devote an undue amount of time and effort to monitoring your actions and that of the trust. It's almost as if they make it a part-time job. My experience suggests that those types of beneficiaries are often unemployed, or underemployed.

Nagging Beneficiaries

You will no doubt encounter know-it-all beneficiaries who believe they understand and know how to administer the trust and its assets in different and better ways than you can. Likewise, you'll have beneficiaries who are nagging and constantly bar raging the trustee with inquiry after inquiry that soon pass the point of polite relevance. Dealing with such beneficiaries and inquiries is part of the trustee's job and how to handle those are best left to a trustee, and their counsel, on an individual and case-by-case basis.

To be clear: the inquiries of the beneficiary need to be professionally and politely met with a response in a timely manner.

Dealing with nagging beneficiaries is part of your job.

If you don't like dealing with them, there is a remedy for you: *resign*.

Just because a beneficiary may be overly inquisitive or constantly sending emails to you does not mean that you owe them any less of a duty.

Your job is to serve.

The law does not impose a different standard on trustees for those beneficiaries who you believe are taking up too much of your time. If you truly believe that a beneficiary is taking up an undue amount of your time, you might speak to your trust counsel about altering your compensation so that you are paid, at least in part, for the time that you spend communicating to the beneficiaries. This would, however, require you to keep detailed time records and to track with accuracy the amount of time and dates which you spend communicating with particular beneficiaries.

Best Practices

Experienced trustees will provide written responses to beneficiary inquiries and retain copies of all communications and documents and other information which are provided to beneficiaries. Consider summarizing the substance of telephone calls and communications with beneficiaries so that there is a clear written record of what was discussed. This will also provide the beneficiary with an opportunity to correct your recollection or understanding if they believe it to be inaccurate. Other than perfect recollection or memory, which is rare, nothing is more accurate than, and certainly courts give great credence to, contemporaneous writings which memorialize conversations. So, write it down – when the conversation is present and fresh in your memory.

In today's society, communications via US mail are no longer necessary except perhaps to obtain a return receipt. Email communications are satisfactory and are indeed the norm now. Faxes have become virtually obsolete. But be sensitive to particular requirements in the jurisdiction which governs the administration of the trust. There may be specific requirements for the dissemination of trust information by return receipt, personal delivery, or the use of commercial delivery service.

Fraud

This is important. Failure to disclose may be a form of fraud. There are many types of fraud in the law. Fraud is not limited to stealing or running a Ponzi scheme. Fraud includes:

- Failure to disclose information when you have a duty to do so
- Hiding the ball
- Mis-stating facts, or being misleading
- Providing only partial facts, or telling half-truths

Don't open yourself up to a lawsuit for breach of trust, or fraud, because you are not disclosing.

Example:

Let's say a trustee discloses that the trust paid $100,000 as a brokerage fee for the sale of real estate. In truth, the real estate broker was a friend of the trustee who kicked back $80,000 to the trustee under the table. The kickback is not disclosed to the beneficiaries. Five years later, the trustee is replaced with a bank or corporate institution. The prior trustee is released and discharged from liability by all the beneficiaries. Two years after the corporate trustee takes over, it, for the first time, discovers the $80,000 kickback from the real estate broker to the trustee which occurred seven years ago. In other words, two years into the corporate trustee's tenure was the first opportunity for the corporate trustee to know of the fraud. The corporate trustee, seven years after the fraud, may be permitted to seek damages against the prior trustee.

Disclosure May Mean More Than You Think

At first glance, one might believe that the duty of disclosure is a no-brainer.

I can't tell you how many times individual trustees tell me that they didn't know:

- They were supposed to disclose something
- They did not know the beneficiary was entitled to certain information
- They didn't think disclosure pertained to certain information or a particular transaction.

Non-disclosure is a common and recurring problem for many individual trustees. Whether due to impatience, or perhaps lack of attention, many fail to disclose. Some may not want to deal with, or hire, an attorney. Whatever the reason, non-disclosure has to stop. No hiding the ball. And remember: if you start to get "sneaky" and purposely don't disclose something, or tell only half the story, or don't disclose something entirely accurately, that's bad: really bad. As you just read, that can be fraud.

I, personally, have always viewed the role of a trustee as a role that is important, honorable and noble. Somebody, either the grantor, beneficiaries, or a court of law, has asked you to serve in this fiduciary role. You've been reposed with great trust and confidence, and in some cases, it is no exaggeration to say that the finances and fortunes of some beneficiaries lie in your hands. It is an awesome responsibility. Although you should certainly be entitled to a certain amount of respect and deference, you should also be humbled by this role and understand your duties and those you serve. Control freaks need not apply. For those with attitudes and an unrealistic sense of self-worth: ditch the attitude.

Minor Beneficiaries

If a beneficiary is a minor, you should provide notice and accountings and relevant information to parents. If there are no parents, provide the information to the legal (court appointed) guardian. If there is no court appointed guardian, you need to get one so that someone may protect the minor's rights.

Once the minor beneficiary attains majority, you should no longer share that beneficiary's information with their parents unless you are instructed to by the beneficiary. Check the trust's governing laws to know whether majority is age 18 or 21. You are required to provide information and to account to the beneficiary who is now an adult – regardless whether you believe that beneficiary may be irresponsible. Ignore the demands from parents who don't want you to send trust information to the beneficiary.

You will, no doubt, be implored, pleaded with, and even threatened by persons who don't want a young beneficiary to learn of his or her trust. They will argue that it is in the beneficiary's best interests not to inform them of the trust or the value of the assets. You should be listening to your trust counsel, and not pleads from third parties who are strangers to the trust. In truth the decision of who receives trust information has already been made. The decision was made by the grantor, when he or she created the trust which may have provisions for providing information and accountings. The legislature or the courts instruct you on who you must provide information to.

Steps You Learned

1. You have an ongoing duty to provide relevant information to your beneficiaries

2. Keep accurate records: hire a trust accountant

3. Great trust and confidence is placed in you: take your duties seriously or take the highway

4. No hiding the ball!

5. Account every year

Responsibility, Impartiality & Good Faith

Your duties go as far as always acting with impartiality and in good faith.

What adjectives will your beneficiaries, your attorney, or a judge use to describe you and your tenure as trustee?

Here are some adjectives to describe a good and competent trustee:

- Attentive
- Reflective
- Caring
- Intelligent
- Honest
- Forthright

- Humble
- Advice-seeking
- Inclusive
- Prudent
- Detailed
- Advice-seeker

Here are some adjectives to describe a bad trustee:

- Condescending
- Control freak
- Know-it-all
- Sneaky
- Neglectful
- Biased
- Untimely

- Deceptive
- Sloppy
- Non-responsive
- Late
- Self-dealing
- Frustrating

A trustee's obligations, or duties, include the ongoing duty to act objectively, impartially, and in good faith. They are so important, and must be so clearly understood by a trustee, that they warrant discussion. They are important and cannot be overlooked, suspended or ignored. They must be at the forefront of your thoughts.

> At all times, and without exception, a trustee must place the interests of the beneficiaries above everyone else's —including the trustee's own.

More recently, within the last 10 years, there've been a striking number of changes to trust law which were once thought unimaginable; including more clearly defined rights for beneficiaries, the use of third parties (trust protectors, investment agents, and designated recipients of information), expanded jurisdiction for courts, increased power and discretion for judges to intervene in the administration of trusts and also the opportunity to re-write the terms of an irrevocable trust through a court action called "reformation."

Nevertheless, one central tenet has remained unchanged: you, as trustee, are a fiduciary who is charged with looking out for, protecting and acting solely in the best interests of the beneficiaries according to the governing law and the grantor's intent as expressed in the language of the trust document.

In fact, if you are reading this far, chances are that you have already agreed to do this.

At all times, and without exception, a trustee must place the interests of the beneficiaries about everyone else's – including your own. This duty is 24/7 – no breaks, and no holidays. And no excuses.

Think of a trustee as a trusted individual who is holding the hands of a person, a beneficiary, who is blindfolded and unable to see a clear path in front. It is your obligation to look out for, and guide, that beneficiary – to make sure that no harm comes to them.

Trustees get into trouble when they are biased, they improperly favor one beneficiary over another, make decisions for their own, personal reasons or beliefs, and not out of care or prudence. Don't place your own self-interests, and personal feelings, above your obligation to serve the beneficiaries. If you exhibit disdain for, animosity towards, or lack of interest in, a beneficiary, then that is when your objectivity and good faith are gone. And at that time, it is time for you to go.

Treat Each Beneficiary Equitably: Even If The Trust Document Permits Un-Equal Distributions

The trust document may permit distributions to be made in different amounts for various beneficiaries. Different standards for distribution should not cause a trustee to believe that any particular beneficiary is less important than another. Each and every beneficiary needs to be treated fairly and certainly according to the standards and terms set out by the grantor in the trust document.

> Trustees must treat each beneficiary equitably, or fairly, although the standards for distribution may be different, and the actual amounts of money distributed to beneficiaries are not the same (unequal).

Example:

A trust document may state that during the lives of 2 brothers "...*the trustee shall distribute all of the income to Brother A and the trustee may distribute principal to or for*

Brother A's health, education, maintenance and support, as the trustee determines is necessary or proper from time to time."

That same trust document may also state that *"...the trustee shall distribute principal for Brother B, for his health, education, maintenance, support,* **and comfort** *specifically including for the use of a new vehicle every three years, for the renting of a summer house for family vacations, for travel and entertainment and lifestyle expenses in a manner to which Brother B has become accustomed to as of the date of the execution of the trust document, and also for the purchase of a larger residence should Brother B get married, or have children."*

Issue: Do you treat the brothers equally?

Answer: No. The standards for distribution for Brother B are clearly more giving than those for Brother A. They are more specific, more detailed; suggesting that the grantor intended to, or anticipated that the trustee should, distribute more money to B than A. The document appears to acknowledge or enunciate the grantor's intent or desire that trust funds be used not just for necessities, but also for Brother B's lifestyle, or enjoyment—his "comfort." The criteria which the trustee shall use in determining whether to distribute, or not distribute, principal for Brother A and Brother B are different. But, at all times, the trustee must treat both brothers impartially, objectively, and fairly, and equitably—even though the dollar amount to each may be different, perhaps substantially different.

Marital Trusts And The Tension Between "Income" And "Remainder" Beneficiaries

Example: Consider a marital trust, where all the income shall be distributed annually to the surviving spouse, and the trustee may distribute principal for the spouse's benefit. Upon the spouse's death, all trust funds shall be distributed to the grantor's son from a prior marriage. The grantor and his spouse were longtime clients of the West Palm Beach Bank & Trust Company, where surviving spouse has had her individual or personal banking for 15 years. The surviving spouse serves as co-trustee with the bank, and has demanded that high-yielding, income-producing assets, such as REITs, junk bonds, and high dividend paying securities, constitute 90% of the trust portfolio, with the remaining 10% being cash. The bank purchases a number of high yielding investments haphazardly which they disclose to the remainder beneficiary, the grantor's son from a prior marriage.

"Really, Dad? I get the money when she is gone?!?! You're 75, your current wife is 20 years younger than I am. My actuary says that will be 23 years after I am dead!!!!"

Is this investment "thesis" objective? Impartial? Of course not. In this example, the two co-trustees are "chasing yield" without regard to safety of principal, and without regard to their obligation to consider growth and capital appreciation as an as an element of their investment plan for the trust as a whole. While there is no doubt that during the surviving spouse's life she is the sole and exclusive beneficiary of the trust, the trustees cannot invest without concern for the remainder beneficiary. We all understand that everyone likes money. But any prudent investment plan must include a strategy which balances current yield, or income, as well as safety of principal and reasonable capital appreciation (growth) over an extended period of time.

The co-trustees invested imprudently, with a misplaced, risky, short-term goal that clearly and selfishly favored the surviving spouse to the detriment of the remainder beneficiary. Objective? No. Impartial? No.

The irony is that by choosing the investments which they did, the co-trustees exposed the trust assets to unnecessary risk which could have, over time, greatly diminished her income stream. The other irony is that they could have employed one or more methods to increase the distributions to her, most prob ably at a lower income tax rate, while still investing prudently and with care for the remainder beneficiary, and with greater safety of principal. It may be possible to convert the spouse's income interest to a "unitrust" percentage or otherwise "adjust" (move) principal to "income." Ideally, this gets more money to the spouse and permits the trustee to invest (more) for growth, benefitting the remainder beneficiaries.

As trustee, it will be your job, from time to time, to save co-trustees, and beneficiaries, from themselves.

> "Fair" does not mean "equal."

Partially Does Not Mean Equally

There is a common misunderstanding that impartiality means treating all the beneficiaries the same. It doesn't. It means there is no favoritism. No undue, un-deserved benefits or advantage. This duty of impartiality does not mean that you ignore the plain language of the trust, nor the grantor's intent.

Remember, fair does not always mean equal.

Impartiality does not always equate with equality. The trustee should not look for an easy way out. The trustee should not necessarily seek acquiescence, or approval, in place of exercising sound discretion and judgment.

If The Grantor Wanted To Treat Everyone Equally, He Or She Would Have Done So

The trustee has a responsibility to be fair, objective, and impartial. These duties cannot be shelved, or placed on hold. A trustee is required to be ever-vigilant to its responsibilities, and to the duties which it has agreed to uphold.

Many parents, grantors of trusts, wish to treat loved ones and beneficiaries equitably, but not necessarily equally. If the grantor of a trust, under all circumstances, wanted each and every one of the beneficiaries to receive precisely equal distributions of trust funds, the grantor would have clearly enunciated this in the trust document.

Example:

The trust may read: *"All distributions to my three children shall at all times and in all respects be of equal dollar amounts. Should my trustee choose to make a distribution to one beneficiary, the trustee shall make equal distributions at the same time and in the same amount to all other beneficiaries."*

But this is not the case. In fact, most grantors **want** their beneficiaries to be treated differently. That's why discretion is given.

After all, different beneficiaries are going to have various demands and needs, different sources of income and stages of wealth. One of the purposes of having a trust is to provide flexibility to the trustee to provide for the different needs of the various beneficiaries from time to time.

Would You Let The Prisoners Run The Jail?

You need to remember why the grantor placed money in trust in the first place: The grantor has refused to throw money in the laps of his or her beneficiaries.

The grantor may love the beneficiaries, but just doesn't trust them to be financially responsible. Or, put another way, the grantor did not intend, did not want, to have wealth used in ways they found dis-approving.

Rather, the grantor has set up a relationship, the trust: with standards of distribution—and standards of non-distribution.

In other words, the trustee should not be distributing trust funds for the sake of distributing money. Trust distributions should only be made when the standards for distribution are satisfied.

Example:

Consider a large trust which has a number of beneficiaries each with various spending habits, annual incomes, and needs. One beneficiary makes regular requests of the trustee for sizable chunks of principal from the trust. In short, this beneficiary is always asking for money.

Issue: How is a trustee to act?

Answer 1: A good trustee will examine the request for principal, consider it, gather any information which may be necessary or helpful, to make a determination whether it should be granted or not. A distribution would only be made if it were in line with the grantor's intent as expressed in the document.

Answer 2: A bad trustee may seek acquiescence of the beneficiaries rather than exercising the judgment which the grantor expected. Many times, a trustee will poll the beneficiaries and inform them of the request for principal distribution. Often, the other beneficiaries will consent to the distribution as long as an equal distribution is made to them. Everyone agrees, and the trustee then makes distributions to all beneficiaries. Wrong.

The prudent administration of a trust is not "tit-for-tat".

Equal is not necessarily fair, nor impartial, nor objective, nor in tended. Mutual acquiescence by beneficiaries is not the way to administer a trust. If the grantor wanted that, he or she would have made each beneficiary a co-trustee. In this example, in stead of independently exercising its discretion and judgment, the trustee, in essence, has thrown its responsibility out the window, and permitted the beneficiaries to serve as trustee and decide how much they should get.

Don't let the prisoners run the jail cell. Exercise discretion in a sound, thought-out manner.

The Spendthrift Child

Ever know a child, friend or relative who just never had enough? Who always seemed to spend whatever funds they had?

Example:

Consider a $12 million family trust whose terms permit the trustee to distribute income or principal for the benefit of the surviving spouse, and also the grantor's three adult daughters. Upon the death of the surviving spouse, the trust terminates, and the entire trust shall be distributed in equal shares to the three daughters. Each of the three daughters is in good health and is expected to survive the surviving spouse. The surviving spouse has sufficient personal (non-trust) funds. Distributions from the trust to the surviving spouse are not anticipated.

One of the three daughters is a spendthrift, who has repeatedly asked for six-figure distributions each and every year, which the trustee has granted. The other two daughters have made no requests for distributions from the trust.

Issue: After years of seeing money leave the trust for the benefit of the spendthrift, her two sisters are sick and tired of this and want it to stop. Is it fair for the two daughters to, in essence, subsidize the spending habits of the spendthrift? Because that is exactly what the trustee is doing – placating the spendthrift with her sisters' money. How?

Currently, any distribution today for the spendthrift daughter is a decrease in the expected inheritance of all three daughters. If the trustee distributes one dollar to the spendthrift daughter today, it's as if one third is being distributed from each of the three daughters' future trust shares.

Answer: What the trustee should have done, to be fair and impartial, would have been to presently (now) divide the trust into three separate shares, one for each daughter. All three shares could be used, if necessary, for the benefit of the surviving spouse. Upon the death of the surviving spouse, each daughter's share would be distributed to the respective daughter. However, during the life of the surviving spouse, any distributions for the benefit of one of the three daughters would come only from their individual share – and not from the entire trust fund. Those distributions for the spendthrift daughter would only diminish her share – and not her sisters'.

You are required to act responsibly. You must evaluate requests, and data, and make decisions. Make judgment calls. You must exercise discretion and sound, independent, judgment. This does not mean that you say "yes" to each beneficiary, but it also means that you not be ever-defiant, negative, or antagonist.

And by all means, don't be a jealous trustee.

The Jealous Trustee

As the trustee, you cannot substitute your lifestyle or your spending habits, and your financial limitations, for the grantor's intent or for those of the particular beneficiary you have agreed to serve. This is a polite way of saying if you are not as rich as the grantor or beneficiary, don't be jealous. Be a good trustee.

A trustee is a service provider, but not a servant.

I can remember working for a Palm Beach trust company, and sitting on the committee which evaluated requests for discretionary principal distributions for beneficiaries. It was our job to evaluate beneficiaries' requests and to exercise our discretion. One trust officer did not make a lot of money, and did not lead a lavish lifestyle. She did not wear designer clothing, did not vacation in exotic places, she did not drive luxury automobiles. But she did have a say on trust distributions.

The trust permitted discretionary distributions for the beneficiaries' "lifestyle." This trust beneficiary wanted money for something – I can't remember. I just remember that it did not seem outlandish. And the discretionary language was broad.

We discussed the request and whether a distribution would be proper. I can still remember the trust officer's negative, even antagonistic, and condescending rebuke of the beneficiary's request.

"I'm not going to give her money for that!" the trust officer exclaimed. From the trust officer's tone and facial expres-

sion, and attitude, it was clear that the trust officer was jealous.

The trustee must act with undivided loyalty for each of the beneficiaries, and for the trust as a whole. A trustee should remain nonpolitical and objective at all times, even in the face of a lifestyle or choices which may be personally disapproving.

> Would you distribute funds to a beneficiary for an abortion or medical marijuana?

Conflicts Of Interest And Acts Of Self-Dealing

The trustee must avoid all conflicts of interest, even the appearance of a conflict of interest, and certainly avoid any and all acts of self-dealing. Conflicted transactions and acts of self-dealing are either void or voidable under the law and will subject a trustee to damages, interest, attorneys fees and costs, surcharge, and removal.

Example:

A client's long time attorney drafts a trust for the client, which names the attorney as trustee. After client dies, the trust administration begins. The trustee sells a piece of real estate once believed to have been worth $2 Million for $10 Million. The trustee does not provide annual accountings to the beneficiaries and takes a $1 Million "trustee fee", which he did not disclose. The trustee also paid $70,000 to his law firm for "attorneys fees".

Issue: Is the secret fee of $1 Million reasonable and could the trustee employ his own law firm?

Answer: No.

Steps You Learned

1. Be fair and equitable

2. Understand the interplay between "income" beneficiaries and "remainder" beneficiaries

3. Trust distributions are not "tit" for "tat": equal is not always correct

4. Don't let your emotions or personal feelings rule the day

5. Avoid conflicts of interests and do not engage in acts of self-dealing

7

What's Mine is NOT Yours!

You do not own the trust property; your interest is as a protector – to manage the trust property for the exclusive benefit of the beneficiaries.

The trust property is not your own. So don't treat it like yours. Ever.

You must respect the integrity of the trust, itself, the relationship of a trustee to the beneficiaries, as well as the trust property.

The trust is a distinct legal entity, in many ways like a corporation. You don't own the trust assets and can't run it like you administer your own personal assets. After all, Tim Cook, the CEO of Apple, doesn't own Apple, even though he runs it. Apple belongs to the shareholders, even though

Cook may be a shareholder. A trust belongs to the beneficiaries, even though you may be a trustee and also a beneficiary. You can't run the trust anyway you want it.

In legal jargon, you, the trustee, are said to hold or possess "legal title" to the trust property for the beneficiaries, who have an equitable interest in the property. In other words, you, as trustee, will appear as record owner of any property.

That means your name as trustee would appear on all account statements for trust assets which are held at a financial institution, such as a brokerage account. You, as trustee, would complete the account application and any account opening documents for such a financial account. Your name should not appear alone on the documents and statements. Those documents should reflect your capacity as trustee. For example: "John Pankauski, as Trustee of the 2013 Pankauski Family Trust".

For trust-owned real estate, your name would be on the deed, or on any real estate tax bill, and in any property records – as trustee. Costs and expenses related to trust-owned real estate, such as insurance or maintenance fees, would be billed to you, as trustee. But you don't own the real estate, any more than you are personally responsible for the insurance or maintenance fees associated with the trust real property. The trust owns the real estate. You, as trustee, hold legal title to it. You are the record owner. If you sign documents, or a deed to convey any property, you will do so "As Trustee".

You are, in some sorts, a guardian of the property and the rights and interests of the beneficiaries. You are more than a custodian because you are not merely holding assets for another and awaiting further instructions: you actually make the decisions and give the instructions. A custodian or depository (like a bank or brokerage firm) holds assets for you. And you manage those assets and make the decisions on what to do with those assets – for the benefit of the beneficiaries.

As has been discussed, your one goal, and one duty, is to protect and advance the interests of the beneficiaries and the trust as a whole. You should not personally or individually advance your own interests or profit from this relationship, other than to receive reasonable compensation for your service.

> You cannot do as you please with the trust property, or as you might do, as if the trust property were your own.

You must remember that the trust funds are not your own. You cannot do as you so please with the trust property, or as you might do, if it were your own. If, for example, you personally thought that gold is a great investment, you could not, should not, invest the *entire* trust portfolio in gold just because you may have invested your own personal funds in gold. You should construct a well-balanced, diversified portfolio which is attuned to the short-term and long-term goals of the trust, risk tolerances of the beneficiaries, and which has a plan or strategy for short-term cash needs and yield as well as long-term appreciation of capital. *"But, I bought gold for my personal account"* is no investment strategy. It is not a justification for speculating with trust assets, and it never gets you out of trouble. What you do with your own assets or personal investments is irrelevant.

You can't loan yourself money from the trust even if it's for a very short period of time, and even if you pay back the trust with a wonderful rate of interest. Such a loan would be an act of self-dealing and a misuse of trust funds which would justify your removal as trustee as well as a surcharge or fine against you personally. Go to a bank – not the trust.

You Can't Use Trust Funds For Personal Purposes

During the boom times, everybody seems to love real estate and God knows everyone thinks they're an expert on real estate. As this book goes to press, Florida, and the nation, seem to be experiencing, a small rebound in real estate demand and prices, from the lows of the Great Recession. In Florida, there is a saying that the history of real estate is either "boom or bust". So let's use real estate as an example.

Example:

A proposed development looks to be a very exciting, successful project. You, personally, place a deposit with the developer to purchase a pre-construction unit. On a return visit, you speak to the sales manager about purchasing another unit. You also consider purchasing two units for a trust for your nephews. The salesperson informs you that if you buy three more units right now she is able to offer a sizable discount that will not be available at a later date. You're in: you wire funds from the trust account for the down payment for the three preconstruction units – two for the trust and another one for you.

By 9:00 AM the next day, you have refunded your down payment to the trust, plus interest.

Issue: That's OK, right?

Answer: No. It's not. By using trust funds to purchase a unit for yourself, you have breached your fiduciary duty, engaged in a conflicted transaction, and in an act of self-dealing. **The trust assets are for your nephews' use, not yours.** It doesn't matter that you "borrowed" the trust funds for a very short period of time, or that you paid above-market interest to the trust. Trustees don't use trust funds for personal investments. The trust is not your ATM, your banker or your lender.

From a damage standpoint, since you've refunded the funds plus interest, it appears that the trust was not financially damaged. It is been made whole monetarily. However, in a non financial manner, the trust has been damaged: you engaged in a prohibited transaction. You used trust funds for your personal use or gain, and not for the benefit of the beneficiaries. This is an absolute violation of your duty of loyalty, and your ongoing duty to be a fiduciary, and to avoid conflicted transactions and to refrain from acts of self-dealing.

Keep Trust Funds Segregated

Keep trust funds and assets separate and segregated from your own personal funds. Don't commingle your personal assets with trust assets. Don't put trust funds, dividend checks, matured CDs, etc. into your checking account.

Even if you use interest or dividends or sale proceeds to pay trust expenses or your compensation, deposit those funds in a trust account and then pay expenses and pay yourself by a separate check or distribution which clearly identifies its purpose.

Trust assets should be clearly identified and in unique, separate and distinct accounts. Any time your name appears on a statement, on an invoice, or any type of property record, it should be followed by the words "as trustee" in the title, followed by the title of the trust, or description of the trust.

Protect Trust Property

You must always protect the trust property. You cannot "leave be" the trust assets. You must collect and reinvest them, protect them from loss, and act in a manner necessary to preserve and hopefully grow the trust balance.

> Don't ignore the terms found in the trust document. They are not suggestions.

Example:

One spouse dies. She created two trusts, a marital trust and a family trust, and names her surviving spouse as the sole trustee of both trusts. The terms of both trusts state that the surviving spouse may not receive funds from the family trust until the entire marital trust has been depleted.

Issue: The surviving spouse, in good faith, withdraws money from the family trust when the marital trust has $500,000 in it. Was the withdrawal from the family trust acceptable?

Answer: No. A trustee does not have discretion to deviate from very clear trust language. Don't ignore the document's plain language. After all, the language in the trust document is not a suggestion. It was an instruction. And when you agreed to serve as trustee, you promised to follow instructions.

Was This Real Estate Deal The Best Way To Get Exposure To The Real Estate Market?

Chapter 8 deals with a trustee's duty to invest prudently, but the pre-construction real estate example used earlier in this chapter is a good one to start thinking about how to invest as a trustee. Perfection is not expected. Failure to plan is not justified.

In our example, the trustee wanted to invest his nephews' trust in pre-construction units. If real estate was an appropriate investment, you need to convince me that that specific development was better than other real estate investments.

- Did you research your real estate options?
- Are there other developments?
- Did you employ a broker?
- Why not invest in a handful of the highest quality publicly traded REITs?
- Or a REIT mutual fund with an outstanding manager?
- Or a low-cost, low fee REIT index fund?

To justify investing in this one particular preconstruction project, you would need to specifically understand why this project, with this developer, in this geography, at this time, is worth the risk of investing trust assets – and then be able to justify why this project is a better investment than the alternatives. Can you explain how the risk of investing in this project is less than the alternatives, and why the expectation of return is higher? Can you say that the trust investment will be less risky and likely to produce greater returns?

Can you picture Dana Carvey impersonating President George H. W. Bush and saying: "Wouldn't be prudent."?

Steps You Learned

1. Don't treat trust property like your own

2. Keep trust funds separate from your own

3. Respect the institution of the trust

4. Understand your role as a guardian or protector of trust property

5. Read – and understand – the trust document

The Prudent Investor: What's Your Plan?

Invest as a prudent investor would; not as you personally want or how you think you should invest.

Everyone knows that a trustee must be "prudent".

Few, however, seem to really comprehend what this means.

Truth be told, you could write an entire book on how trustees should invest. Until then, this chapter will focus on the broad highlights of investing trust assets with a few examples thrown in, which appear to be recurring problems.

The Prudent Investor Rule

The term "prudent man rule" comes from an 1830 Massachusetts case by the name of Harvard College and Massachusetts General Hospital v. Amory. This case enunciates the standard of conduct of one who invests funds for another. As the court explained: *"All that can be required of a trustee to invest, is, that he shall conduct himself faithfully and exercise a sound discretion. He is to observe how men of prudence, discretion and intelligence manage their own affairs, not in regard to speculation, but in regard to the permanent disposition of their funds, considering the probable income, as well as the probable safety of the capital to be invested."*

Over time, the prudent "man" rule has become the prudent "investor" rule and the concepts found in the Amory case have served as the starting point for fiduciary investing and is now, along with Modern Portfolio Theory, the backbone for individual states' prudent investor statutes.

> The law is exacting in its scrutiny of your conduct as trustee.

What we take away from the Amory case is that the courts, indeed the law, place a great burden and responsibility on those who invest assets for another. The law is exacting in its scrutiny of your conduct as trustee. The law presumes – indeed demands – that you will be prudent. The law does not expect you to be Warren Buffet, or some Wall Street whiz, but it does demand that you will bring to the table a reasonable amount of attention, diligence, concern, and yes, even skill. If you don't have those traits, you need to hire someone who does or you need to resign. You cannot invest a trust's funds haphazardly. You need to have a plan or strategy.

A Rule Of Conduct

In determining whether a trustee is prudent or not, the law will examine your conduct, and not necessarily your investment returns. The prudent investor rule is a rule of conduct: how you as a trustee are acting or not acting—how you acted, or failed to act. Investment returns, or lack of investment returns, may be a gauge of damages, but do not necessarily indicate prudence or imprudence.

"My trustee lost 20% this quarter and she has the gall to tell me that the trust portfolio is doing better than the S&P 500 Index. What about the make-me-money index?"

For example, assume a trustee invests all trust assets in gold, and the value triples over six months (when the S&P 500 was up 10%). The trustee was not prudent. The fact that the trust assets tripled is only relative to the issue of damages. The trustee invested all the assets in one shot, in one asset class, in one investment – undiversified, highly risky, and a concentration. You don't put all your investment eggs in one basket. You don't go to Vegas and put all the trust assets on red.

The trustee's conduct was improper, and would warrant removal – even though there may be no monetary damage. A 200% return is not a defense. Prudence is measured by conduct, not basis points, ROI or percentage gains.

Is Cash Really King?

By the same token, consider a trustee who is "nervous about the market and keeps it all in cash for two year while the equity markets have appreciated 4% annually. Absent some type of doomsday scenario, such as a world war, or a threat of one, or extreme cash needs, it is difficult to justify keeping everything in cash for two years.

How much trouble is the trustee in? One of the measures of damages is what a properly managed, prudent investment port folio would have returned over that same period of time. The equity markets returning 4% a year would suggest one damage model, to which you would add interest, costs and perhaps attorneys fees.

There are scenarios which would justify keeping everything in cash, depending on the trust's purpose. Going to cash may make sense to lock in gains, and eliminate investment risk, when, for example, the money will be used to pay tuition or make a final distribution.

View The Portfolio As A Whole

Prudent investing views the trust portfolio as a whole, without necessarily determining whether a particular investment is prudent or imprudent, "good" or "bad".

If individual investments are part of a reasonable, overall investment plan or strategy, and they lose money, that loss will not necessarily have been imprudent.

> Trustees prudently analyze and accept or reject risk. Trustees don't speculate

Remember, the prudent investor rule is a test of conduct, not necessarily return. The law will examine not an isolated investment by the trustee, but rather the totality of the trustee's conduct – what his or her investment plan or strategy was, how that plan or strategy was implemented, and whether that was prudent or not.

> What is important to note, is that this does not give a trustee the freedom to create a "risk pocket" within the trust portfolio or to take a "flyer" with a small amount of the trust assets.

Beneficiaries' Wacky Investment Ideas

It's one thing if an amazing businessperson with an enviable track record of creating successful startups provides you with a limited opportunity to get in on the ground floor of a new business venture. Similarly, if you have access to the finest private equity funds, or hedge funds, or venture capital funds, these are unique investment opportunities that warrant consideration and evaluation. It is quite another story, however, when an unaccomplished trust beneficiary requests a large trust distribution in the guise of an "investment".

Trust beneficiaries are notorious for becoming real estate experts overnight – and asking for trust money for their "flyers". Consider a Florida corporate trustee receiving a request for $1 million from a beneficiary to "invest" in a bed-and-breakfast down in the Florida Keys. The beneficiary has found an old, beautiful "fixer upper" in the Keys, and wants to renovate it, and open a bed-and-breakfast. The beneficiary suggests that this would be a great investment for the trust.

The problem with that, of course, is that the beneficiary doesn't work, is a spoiled rich kid, has never operated a business, has no business plan, and really just wants the money to move to the Keys, walk Duval Street and bask in the sun. Of course, the trustee has to ask itself, or better yet, ask the beneficiary: *"Since I have dozens of investment options at my fingertips, tell me why I should invest the trust assets with you in a fixer upper? If we wanted the trust to be further exposed to the real estate market, why would I invest with you, and not in a low cost REIT index fund?"*

What Is Required To Be A Prudent Investor?

Being prudent is more than just having a diversified portfolio. The prudent investor rule requires a trustee to have a plan or strategy which considers both the production of income and the growth of capital, the income or lifetime beneficiaries, as well as those beneficiaries who take later in time. Investments should not be made haphazardly. An analysis should be conducted. Opportunities should be considered and weighed. The trustee must be able to justify each and every holding in the trust portfolio, how long they anticipate holding such an investment, and what expected range of returns they hope to achieve. In essence, a trustee needs to clearly enunciate why each and every investment was purchased and retained.

Inherited Assets And The Acts Of The Prior Trustee

Trustees have a duty to monitor, on an ongoing basis, the trust's individual holdings. Assets which a trustee "inherits" from a prior trustee need to be evaluated, and you'll need to justify retaining those assets – or selling them. If you cannot justify retaining those, you need to sell them and reinvest the proceeds.

Consider: You are a successor trustee and read a trust statement and see that the prior, outgoing, trustee invested in a smattering of stocks and bonds. So: if you had 100% cash, would you, right now, purchase those assets which the prior trustee invested in? If your answer is "no", then sell. If your answer is "yes", then keep them.

A decision to retain assets is tantamount to a decision to "buy." Whether an investment was purchased yesterday, two years ago, or even 20 years ago, does not matter.

> Monitor. Evaluate. Consider and re-consider.

If you don't want an investment or it does not fit into your plan, then sell it.

While income taxes attributable to a sale may be one factor in considering whether to sell or retain a security, don't let the tax tail wag the dog.

Don't rely on what was done in the past. Analyze and draw your own conclusions now, during your tenure. No finger pointing at the prior trustee.

A successor trustee has a *duty to examine* the actions of the prior trustee. If a prior trustee did something wrong, consider bringing an action for surcharge or damages against the prior trustee, if the prior trustee has not already been discharged and released.

What's Your Sell Strategy?

Trustees need a sell strategy.

- What's your time horizon?
- What's your expected return for each asset?
- What will you do if that return is achieved? Sell? Buy more?
- How much loss do you tolerate?
- When do you exit an investment?

Budgets And Beneficiaries

Trustees often request a budget from a beneficiary to determine how much trust money may be distributed for their benefit, such as health, education, maintenance, or support.

Example:

A surviving spouse who has $2 million of her own liquid assets is the lifetime beneficiary of a $3 million trust created by the now deceased grantor. The terms of the trust require the trustee to distribute all the income annually to the surviving spouse, and authorize the trustee to distribute principal to or for her benefit for health, education, maintenance, and support. The trust also states that the trustee shall consider all other assets and income which the surviving spouse has.

Issue: How much money does the surviving spouse need to live on over a 12-24 month period?

Answer: Before distributing trust funds, you will consider the surviving spouse's $2 million. You should ask the surviving spouse for an annual budget. Once a reasonable amount is determined, then you can invest the $3 million trust in light of the needs of the surviving spouse and your duty to the remainder beneficiaries.

Tension Between Beneficiaries

As you might imagine, a natural "tension" will arise between the lifetime beneficiary and the remainder beneficiaries. One wants immediate income, the other wants money saved and invested for the long term. The tension is heightened when the lifetime beneficiary has his own, personal, wealth, and the trustee is not required to consider that when distributions are requested.

Part of a trustee's job is to safeguard principal and to protect all beneficiaries, including the remainder beneficiaries. This includes anticipating how much the trust's principal may grow to over the life expectancy of the surviving spouse—and how much the trust may be diminished by principal distributions to the surviving spouse. What will the trust principal look like in the future? Will it run out?

Anticipating Growth – And Loss – And Distributions

Trustees should estimate what the value of the trust will grow to over time. What if you have two years of losses? What if there are unforeseen medical expenses? Investments don't always go up. And investment returns vary year to year, as do expenses. Our life expectancy is increasing. The likelihood is that we will be incapacitated before we die, requiring additional assistance and care. As beneficiaries age, the cost of living and health care rise.

The trust could be wiped out if there are large losses or distributions. This is why your analysis or forecast is so important.

It's as simple as creating a spreadsheet with various rates of returns and various distribution amounts from year to year.

Invest and manage wisely so you don't run out of money.

Don't Let The Tax Tail Wag The Dog

The honest truth is that people hate paying taxes. Disdain for paying capital gains taxes is not an investment strategy.

Growth of trust assets, after the payment of fees, expenses, and costs, is an important consideration for trustees. The tax implications may be *a* factor in considering whether to sell an investment or not. This makes sense because, at the end of the day, we want to know the net amount which will actually be staying in the trust portfolio or being distributed to the beneficiaries. After tax and after fee returns are an important gauge for fiduciaries.

However, when there are built-in gains, the fact that you're going to have to pay income tax on those gains should never wag the dog. Income taxes should never, ever, be the overriding or only factor.

Be Afraid. Be Very Afraid: Dangerous Language

Be wary of language in the trust document which instructs you or permits you to retain, indefinitely, a particular asset. Watch out for language which attempts to restrict the way you invest. This language may seem innocent or safe, but it's not. It's a wolf in sheep's clothing.

It's not uncommon to see trust language which instructs the trustee to invest only in high-quality bonds, or which instructs you to never sell a particular security. Do not accept the comfort which such language appears to provide. Courts have rightly viewed such language with suspicion and held trustees account able for following such limitations.

Why? A trustee is appointed or hired to exercise good judgment and sound discretion. You can't be an ostrich and bury your head in the sand. You can't point to a prior trustee, to inherited trust investments, or to the language of the trust document alone, and get a pass. Consider a trust document that instructs the trustee to hold, to retain, and to never sell a specific stock. But companies change. We know that each industry and all stocks have faced difficult economic times, bankruptcies, advanced competition, changing technologies and in some sense obsolescence. If you follow the strict language of the trust document, and don't sell, the trust may be wiped out.

At no time does a trust document, no matter what the language says, permit the trustee to be imprudent or foolish, let alone stupid. When faced with such restrictive language, the trustee is required to exercise good judgment, and seek to reform or modify or change the terms of the trust to take off the "handcuffs". Such a change may be done, depending on the governing law of the trust, by consent of the beneficiaries or by a court of law. One of the easiest things for a trustee to do, one of the most cost-effective, one of the most beneficial to the trust, is for you to march into court, and ask the judge for assistance, because you may have a ticking time bomb.

The trustee is not expected to have a crystal ball or to be able to predict what interest rates will do. The law does not expect you to be a prognosticator. You can't be expected to predict the price of bonds or what the equity markets will do. Since most people don't have the time nor experience to manage wealth, consider delegating investment duties to an investment agent.

Steps You Learned

1. Understand that being "prudent" may mean something different than what you believe it means

2. Have a plan or an investment strategy

3. Perfection is not required, but in-attention, neglect or avoidance will not be tolerated

4. Review and re-review – monitor—on-going investments

5. Carefully scrutinize assets which a prior trustee invested in

6. Balance the interests of beneficiaries who want money now and the remainder beneficiaries who want growth

7. Consider when you want to sell, or exit, an investment

Delegate To An Investment Agent

Hire a bank or professional money manager to invest the trust's assets; the trust pays for the fees.

One of the most intelligent, prudent things that an individual trustee can do is to hire an investment expert – one who can manage and invest the trust's assets.

The act of hiring an investment expert is so important, not only for the trust and its beneficiaries, but also for the trustee, that a chapter dedicated solely to this issue is warranted.

> Most individuals have neither the time, nor the experience, to invest money for others.

Trustees Cannot Delegate Discretion, But May Delegate Investment Functions

A trustee is generally not permitted to delegate his or her discretion to another. In other words, you can't ask someone else to make a judgment call, or impose their discretion in place of your own. After all, you are the trustee. You were selected. You agreed to serve. Your judgment and good sense follow. You make the tough calls.

A trustee, however, may employ professionals, like attorneys and accountants, and also experts to advise on investing.

The trustee may *delegate* all investment functions to an *investment agent*. When permitted and proper, delegation can minimize or eliminate potential liability for investment losses.

Delegation suggests the transfer of all investment functions to an investment agent, who will make the calls on what to purchase, retain or sell. The idea behind this is that by permitting delegation of all investment functions, the trust gets professional money management, and the trustee gets limited liability if the investment agent was properly selected and monitored.

Selecting An Investment Agent

The trustee is required to carefully select the investment agent by using reasonable skill and care. If you need help selecting an investment agent, ask your trust counsel.

Your investment agent should not be a family member or any one with whom you have personal or financial ties – no matter how good an investor that person is believed to be. It's easier to tell you what not to do.

Don't:

- Hire someone just because you trust them
- Hire anyone without experience of investing trust as sets, or investing assets on a discretionary basis
- Hire your neighbor
- Hire someone with little experience
- Hire someone who watches CNBC a lot in their spare time and who reads the Wall Street Journal.

And for God's sake, ***don't*** hire your child, your in-law, step child or lover.

Hire one who invests others' funds as a full time job. Consider hiring a bank or trust company to serve as investment agent.

Any delegation should be in writing, and the investment agent should accept, in writing, the delegation and its scope.

Establishing The Scope Of The Delegation And Monitoring The Investment Agent

You will need to establish the scope and terms of the delegation and define what role the investment agent shall play and how they will work with you. At no time may you delegate investment functions in a way which is contrary to, or inconsistent with, the terms of the trust document.

- Are you going to grant to the investment agent absolute discretion to determine asset allocation, and what percentages of the various asset classes will comprise the trust portfolio?

- Are you going to let the investment agent select the individual securities or funds?

- Are you going to limit the scope of the investment agent?

Assuming you may, and indeed do, delegate, all investment functions to an agent, you need to speak with the agent, and understand what actions he or she wishes to take. They need to understand that a trustee is required to have an investment plan or strategy to comply with the prudent investor rule.

You, as trustee, will still be required to monitor the work of the investment agent on an on-going basis. Ostriches need not apply. You can't just throw the investments into the lap of the agent and throw up your hands. You need to periodically review performance and also whether the agent is doing what you want him or her to do. If the agent is doing things which are not contemplated by the delegation, you have a duty to stop it. If you want the agent to purchase index funds and a select basket of equities, and she is purchasing options, you need to put a stop to that.

Are You Permitted To Delegate?

This rule permitting a trustee to delegate investment functions certainly varies from state to state and you should check the governing law of the trust administration. Your trust counsel will certainly understand the issues of delegation and methods by which you, as trustee, may be protected from possible li ability, for the investment of the trust assets. Trust counsel can also assist with defining the scope of the delegation. If a state does not permit delegation, or if the trust document suggests that it cannot be done, it may make sense to seek permission of the beneficiaries, or, better yet, a court, to establish a delegation of investment functions.

On a personal note, my passion is making and collecting wine. One of the highest designations which a wine professional may attain is that of "master sommelier" – one with advanced skill and knowledge through both classroom achievement and in depth experience. As one sommelier instructor stated to a class of students: *"If you know a lot about California wine, and a good amount about Bordeaux, you're going to fail."* The point is well taken.

Just as a master sommelier must be an expert in a vast array of wines, wine-making regions, techniques, *terroir*, and food, your investment agent must be competent enough to understand the myriad of investment issues. I hinted at this earlier, but it bears repeating: stay away from relatives. I can't tell you how many "nephews" or "boyfriends" were "hired" to invest the trust assets inappropriately. Knowing a decent amount about investing, the stock market, and watching CNBC each day, falls miserably short. It is difficult for me to imagine an individual who has both the time and the experience to properly manage funds of another. You need to hire an expert.

There are a lot of "financial consultants" and other investment or "wealth professionals" who aren't worth the cost of their embossed and raised business cards or their slick marketing brochures. Many of them are "stock jocks" or salespersons.

While many financial professionals may indeed be knowledge able and savvy, finding a great "financial consultant" is harder that finding a good trust department or bank. Consider trust departments of banks and trust companies themselves with a so-called "open platform".

Many banks and trust companies have the research teams and economists on board to provide advice and commentary about stocks and bonds, the equity markets, interest rates and the economy. If they are truly objective and independent, they will also provide access to other money managers, or suggest other funds, not just their own.

If you need an international component to your portfolio, an open platform investment agent will suggest mutual funds or money managers or index funds which may be appropriate for the trust portfolio – not just the proprietary funds which that investment agent's employer sells. You want an open platform – the opportunity to invest in a host of other funds or money managers – including their competition.

When you are ready to retain an investment agent:

- Interview them
- Talk to them
- Meet each person on their team that may be working with you
- Meet the portfolio managers who will be doing the actual investing
- Meet the account officers or relationship managers who will be handling the day-to-day
- Ask them how long their average client stays with them

- How large is their average portfolio?

Costs And Fees

You have an ongoing duty to keep compensation and costs reasonable – including that of your investment agent. Various sources suggest that the average mutual fund which invests in equities charges anywhere from 1.11 – 1.25% on an annual basis. Compare this to the Vanguard 500 Index fund which invests in the S&P 500 Index and charges .08% annually. That's a huge swing!

Be mindful of fees within fees. The underlying funds which an investment agent might invest in will most probably be in addition to the investment agent's own fees, and your compensation. You need to understand how investment services and products are priced. It will affect how much is reasonable for you to take as compensation. After all, if you are delegating investment authority to an agent, and they are charging, say, .80% annually, can you justify charging a trustee fee of 1% annually? No.

The average annual fee for a bank or trust company to serve as trustee of an account whose value may go up to $3 million is somewhere between .9% and 1.3% annually. As suggested, should you delegate investment authority to an investment agent, your fee for serving as trustee should not be as high as if you *hadn't* hired an investment agent. Had you retained the authority over all investment functions, there's more work for you to do. By delegating to an investment agent, you are doing less work and, supposedly, incurring less liability. So, frankly, you shouldn't get paid as much.

No double dipping! You can't hire an investment agent who charges the trust 1% to invest that $5 Million trust and you also take a 1% fee. Be reasonable. Pigs get fat but hogs get slaughtered.

Be mindful of smaller banks which offer you a discount off their published fee schedule. Sales persons at banks are hired to get new business – to convince you to use them and not their competitors. They get paid based upon the new revenue that they bring in. While you can negotiate any-thing, including fiduciary fees, be mindful of a sales person who is selling you on price. While cost is a factor, it is merely one factor and less important than the experience, knowledge and service which an investment agent will provide.

Don't sign a fee agreement or other account opening documents without having your counsel read it first. There may be language in there which you don't want. Watch out for arbitration provisions and other terms which may prohibit you from handling disputes in a court of law, or which alter the standard of care which an investment agent should provide to you. Finally, be on the lookout for hidden exit fees and other commissions or costs which may not be reasonable.

Recently, I was hired to negotiate a trustee's fee dispute between a wealthy client and a small bank which wanted a 1% "exit fee" when they were fired. While 1% doesn't seem that awful, it was $100,000 for about a year's work – on top of their management fee! My role was to sue them for "unreasonable" compensation or settle the dispute. I worked. They settled. But if someone had read the account opening documents prior to signing them, all this could have been averted.

Steps You Learned

1. Level with yourself: you probably don't have the time or experience to manage money

2. Research excellent money managers and delegate investment functions to them

3. Monitor the investment agent's work

10

Ready, Aim, Fire!

Why the best day in court may be the one that you avoid.

Trust litigation is a growth industry. People are more apt to question your decisions as a trustee than ever before. Many "lawyer up." Younger generations are more likely to question, investigate, and retain counsel than our parents' or grandparents' generations. Whatever the reasons, a trustee faces the reality of potential disgruntled beneficiaries with each act, buy, sell or hold.

If you make a mistake, or breach your duties, you can be sued and mired in litigation instead of administration. No one wants this. No matter how tough you talk.

If you did something wrong, and you lose the lawsuit, you can be removed as trustee, ordered to pay damages, interest, attorneys fees and costs.

"We met the old fashioned way.
I was his caregiver."

Being a trustee is like being a parent – don't steal from your children, have their best interests at heart, and don't pick favorites, or else they will act out, cost you your time, and harm you financially.

Our firm handles trust litigation. We tell trustees and beneficiaries the same thing: you need to be prepared, both personally (or mentally) and financially, for litigation. You will find it stressful and expensive. And there is no guarantee of the outcome. If you are not ready, litigation is not for you. The same thing holds true for being a trustee. It's a job. Are you ready for it? Really ready for it?

Parents Just Don't Understand: It's Your Children's Trust – Not Yours

Parents support children. Children don't support parents.

That means that you can't use your child's trust fund for your new car. Or to finance a trip to Disney World. Period. No matter how much your new car will be used to comfortably drive your children around, and no matter how safe it will be for them. Children don't purchase cars for parents. No matter how much your children will love Disney World, you have to pay for it: not your children's trust.

Trustees Are Not Bulletproof

Some individual trustees just don't know how much they can lose. At our firm, lawyers advise clients about the potential outcomes to a case. What do your best, and worst, days in court look like? How much can you win or lose? Often, trustees and beneficiaries embroiled in trust litigation don't realize how much they can lose. And they are frightened by the prospect of having to pay thousands and thousands of dollars in attorneys fees to the other side.

As in any damage scenario, if you are found to have breached your fiduciary duty, you normally have to pay back lost profits or damages to the trust. You may also have to pay interest and the other side's attorney's fees. You would probably also have to pay your own attorneys from your own personal funds and not from the trust funds.

Punitive damages are only considered if a trustee has demonstrated outrageous conduct, such that the trustee should be punished. They may be considerably higher than the amount in controversy. However, punitive damages are seldom granted in cases of ordinary negligence. In the trust world, they typically only become an issue when the trustee has stolen funds, misappropriated them, intentionally ignored the trust document, or clearly abused its position of trust or engaged in acts of self-dealing.

The losing side must often pay interest, on top of damages. Interest can be significant and may be payable for a number of years.

Continuing Trustee Wrongs

I previously mentioned that beneficiaries must bring litigation against a trustee within the timeframe called for by the law (the statute of limitations). If a trustee has committed repeated wrongs on a continuing basis, the statute of limitations may not have ended. This means that, at least theoretically, a beneficiary may be able to bring a lawsuit for wrongs committed years ago – and years after a trustee believes the statute of limitations has ended.

You may not be aware that you are doing something wrong. And misguided mistakes can turn into a multiyear continuing tort.

Attorneys Fees

Litigation is expensive. As such, you should carefully analyze your position and your risk of liability if you are accused of wrongdoing. What's the likelihood that you're going to lose?

No matter how successful you are in your own profession or business, and no matter how tough you talk, you will find disputes and litigation stressful. I don't think I have ever had a trustee tell me *"Hey, that lawsuit was a blast. Let's do this again sometime."* Litigation is expensive, even when you spend the trust's money, and most people have better things to do with their time than litigate. Once you go down that road, you can't turn back. Disagreements turn into family feuds. Any chance of reconciling is usually gone.

Truth be told, most people don't want to serve as trustee if it will involve litigation. As much as I would like to think my clients like me, I know that, truthfully, they would rather spend less time with me in my office preparing for depositions, or handling discovery, or strategizing for hearings and trials.

The short of it all is that being a trustee is serious business. It involves blood (family) and money. The beneficiary of the trust is probably related to the grantor by blood or marriage. Trust litigation and, yes, even just plain old trust administration, often involves very deep and personal feelings, and perhaps animosities. It also involves money. Sometimes, quite a bit of money. My experience is that blood and money don't mix well. The fight for blood and money is often only rewarding to the attorneys. I doubt that the grantor of the trust intended to make some attorney a trust beneficiary.

Mis-Distributions

If you have distributed funds my mistake, it is your job to get it back.

Example:

The Trust document requires that 20% of the trust assets shall be distributed to a beneficiary upon a certain happening, or as of a certain date. Through a simple, innocent arithmetic error, you distribute too much to the beneficiary: you distribute 23% instead of 20%. Go get it: send written notice to the beneficiary explaining that too much money was distributed, and requesting, or demanding, that it be returned.

Using Refunding Agreements And Receipts

Good news: most states' laws anticipate this. Some states have very specific statutes which require the beneficiary to return to the trust the excess distribution. However, a good practice for a trustee is, prior to distribution, the beneficiary signs a receipt and re-funding agreement. The beneficiary agrees to return any amount incorrectly distributed, upon notice. It's simple, straightforward, and merely reflects basic law: you can't keep what is not yours, even if the distribution was a mistake.

The question for you, the trustee, is who is responsible for any loss in value? Or, what if the beneficiary has already spent the money or doesn't have it? Who makes the trust whole?

Reliance On Experts May Exonerate You

If you reasonably rely on certain, limited, experts, then, depending on the governing law of your trust, a trustee may be exonerated from certain losses or acts. This is because in certain limited situations, a trustee may only be responsible if he or she was personally at fault. Relying on advice of counsel, or an investment agent, or other expert, may or may not exonerate you, depending on the governing law and the facts. But the point of this is important.

Hiring competent advisors, investment agents, accountants, and attorneys, is the best way to assist you in the performance of your job as trustee and, selfishly, the best way to insulate you from potential liability. Your failure to retain experts, may, itself, be a breach of your fiduciary duty. So, start with a competent and experienced trust counsel and consider adding members to your team, such as a CPA, and an investment agent, with trust experience. Disclose your hiring of them to the beneficiaries, and, if the beneficiaries object to your hiring experts, it's better that this issue be resolved now, rather than years, and thousands and thousands of dollars, down the line.

Trust Language And Consents Don't Always Remove Liability: Even If It Seems Clear On Its Face

Previously, we discussed trust language which may appear to exonerate a trustee from retaining an asset concentration indefinitely. Be mindful of exoneration clauses. Overly broad, trustee-serving language which purports to exonerate a trustee from "all liability" or which simply states that a trustee shall never be liable for damages, would probably be dismissed by a court of law as invalid. That language will not save you from acts of self-dealing, conflicts of interest, intentional torts, such as fraud, or civil theft, and probably not save you from simple negligence, or breaches of your fiduciary duty.

A consent by a beneficiary may or may not exonerate a trustee from breaching their fiduciary duty. At the risk of sounding overly broad, it really depends on what the beneficiary knew, and when they knew it. Remember, you always have the duty of exercising good judgment and sound discretion. You can't delegate your discretion or judgment to beneficiaries. If you get all the beneficiaries to consent to something stupid, or harmful, this consent may not exonerate you at a later date, or in the future or from another beneficiary, or from a judge. Bottom line: don't stick a piece of paper in front of the beneficiary asking them to hold you harmless. While consents may be valid in certain circumstances, they also may not be worth the paper they are printed on.

Staying On As Trustee

The decision of whether to be or remain a trustee is a tough one. You may view compensation as a reason to serve, but you must realize the risks involved. If you are an honest, prudent individual with management and investment skills, this may be the perfect role for you. However, if you are a control freak and cannot separate your personal interests from those of the trust and its beneficiaries, you may find yourself in a heap of trouble. If a dispute comes to litigation, the court will review all of your duties and compare the risks and your actions which you took to those of a reasonable trustee with like skills and knowledge.

"Not only am I younger than my latest wife's adult children, but they are going to flip when they read the trust."

One of your duties as trustee is a duty of confidentiality. Avoid providing information to ones other than those you are legally required to provide it to. "Family friends" or "advisors" or a divorced parent's boyfriend or girlfriend are nothing more than strangers to the trust. Don't post on social media.

In the end, I advise you to evaluate, sincerely, and honestly, why you want to be trustee. Do you have the skill-set, time, and experience? Are you serving for the right reasons? Will your personal feelings cloud your good judgment and objectivity? My advice to you is to leave the role of trustee for the experts: the banks and trust companies. If you insist on serving as trustee, retain trust counsel, and a trust company.

Steps You Learned

1. Trust litigation is now, sadly, commonplace

2. The law permits you to protect yourself, as you work for the benefit of your beneficiaries

3. Damages in a trust lawsuit can be costly

4. Attorneys fees in trust litigation are expensive

5. The losing party to a trust lawsuit may end up paying the other side's attorneys fee, contrary to the general "American" rule that each party to a lawsuit pays their own fees

TIPS

Hiring Trust Counsel

- Interview as many attorneys as you can.

- Seek an attorney whose practice is limited to trust matters.

- Try to find one who handles not just the drafting of trusts, but also the administration and litigation of trust disputes.

- Seek a trust attorney with at least ten years of experience handling trust administration or disputes.

- Ask for references, either clients or other professionals: and call them.

- Beware of the attorney who claims to limit its practice to estate and trust matters, but whose Website also advertises for general litigation, real estate and other areas of the law unrelated to trusts.

- Ask them to describe their involvement (or lack of involvement) with committees and continuing legal education courses of the local and state bar, or the

American Bar Association. Many times, experienced trust counsel are involved with trust committees and are requested to speak or write on trust subjects.

- Inquire how many other pending trust matters he or she is handling right now, as well as how many trust matters his or her firm is involved in.

- Inquire whether the attorney appears regularly in probate court or the judicial division which handles trust disputes. If they are in court regularly, they should know the name of each judge, which floor the judges are located on, what courthouse they are in, and the names of the clerks or judicial assistants. Not knowing this suggests that the attorney isn't one who goes to court much.

- If your attorney guarantees a result to you, or tells you not to worry about who will pay attorneys fees: run.

Conclusion

The use of trusts has exploded. Not surprisingly, as if in lock step, the number of trust disputes has skyrocketed. Trust law is a specialty now. Trust litigation is a subspecialty.

Judges and courts have been granted increased, and very broad, discretion to intervene in the administration of trusts. This means that courts may reform or modify trusts, and their terms, declare rights, suspend or remove a trustee, and do just about anything regarding the trust which justice may require, or which is in the best interests of the beneficiaries or in accordance with the trust creator's intent.

This is an awesome, discretionary power given to judges. Further, individual litigants, such as trust beneficiaries and trustees, may seek court intervention to change the terms of a trust even when a trust may be irrevocable and not "alterable" through relatively new causes of action known as "modification" and "reformation." Yes, if you draft a trust that is "irrevocable", it can be changed.

Just like any other legal field, the world of trusts and trustees has its own particular laws, rules and procedures in each state. Some are enacted by the legislature, reflected in statutes or written laws, and others in binding precedent, that is, reflected in written opinions of courts of law which other courts, and the parties, are required to follow. Not surprisingly, older states such as New York and Massachusetts have a richer body of law and written opinions, or case law.

Other states, such as Florida, may have a smaller body of case law, and a shorter history, but have very progressive, cutting-edge changes to trust law which are reflected in its statutes. In many states, trust statutes may be referred to as the Trust Code, while statutes for estates and probate administration may be referred to as the Probate Code. (While the worlds of trusts and estates are often closely related, they are different. A trustee manages a trust, not an estate. An executor or a personal representative may be in charge of a deceased person's estate.)

The preparation of and drafting of trusts is not only increasingly common but affordable. While some 40 or 50 years ago, and beyond, trusts may have only been used for the ultra rich, the wealthy or the noble few, the legal field of estate planning and will and trust drafting has become an affordable subspecialty. Within the law, it attracts thousands of practitioners who have made trusts available to people across the financial spectrum. While it is common for trusts to contain millions of dollars, leaving property in trust for your loved ones is a common thing not only for the middle or upper middle class, but also for those who leave "only" thousands of dollars.

With the passage of the American Taxpayer Relief Act of 2012, signed on January 1, 2013 by President Obama, estate planning has never been simpler. A married couple may give away during life, or leave at death, a combined $10 million – free of any gift, estate, or inheritance tax (so called "transfer" taxes.) While most people's wealth may be held in a primary residence, an IRA or retirement plan, one's other assets are commonly held, administered and passed along in one's revocable trust (which becomes irrevocable upon the death of the trust creator). Whether you have millions or thousands, your attorney is advising you to use a trust, just as she or he is talking to you about a will, a power of attorney, and health care and guardianship documents.

The new legislation has now clearly shifted the focus for the vast majority of citizens, and, indeed those who advise clients such as trust attorneys, away from tax minimization, to wealth administration: how will your property, your money, be administered, mis-administered, distributed, invested or misused during your life and after your death for your benefit as well as for the benefit of your chosen beneficiaries?

About the Author

John Pankauski, *www.johnpankauski.com*, was born in Salem, Massachusetts, the grandson of Polish and Lithuanian immigrants who arrived in America at the turn of the last century. His parents, products of the Depression and WWII, made a lasting impression on him with their values of hard work and thrift.

John graduated from public schools, a standout lacrosse player, Honor Student, and student athlete at Peabody Veterans Memorial High School. He studied Political Science at the University of Massachusetts at Amherst where he was a member of the Pi Kappa Alpha fraternity, after which he attended Suffolk University Law School in Boston, and later obtained a master's degree in law from the University of Miami School of Law's Graduate Program in Estate Planning. His early career involved sophisticated tax planning and trust administration for wealthy families in Palm Beach, and in the board rooms of some of the most prestigious trust companies.

He founded the Pankauski Law Firm PLLC, *www.pankauskilawfirm.com*, to create a boutique law firm of highly talented professionals which restricts its practice to administration and litigation of family wealth and disputes involving wills, trusts, and estates. In addition to trying cases and handling appeals, the firm defends trustees and advises beneficiaries on their rights related to inheritances, power of attorneys, contested guardianships, investments, and family business interests. He is often asked to mediate complex, highly emotional, family wealth disputes.

John resides in West Palm Beach where he enjoys tennis, softball, following Boston sports teams, cooking, wine, and travel. His passion for wine takes him to Santa Barbara County and Napa often, as well as across the globe, seeking new and interesting wines for his annual Pankauski Pour wine tasting. One of south Florida's premier wine tastings for premium wines, the Pankauski Pour is held each February *www.pankauskipour.com*. The Palm Beach Post named the Pankauski Pour the best small wine event for 2013.

Index